PRISON REFLECTIONS

John Sharp

Dedication

This book is dedicated to my wife, family and friends whose support and love throughout this entire experience has been unwavering. Thank you.

Table of Contents

The Court and to Prison

"I agree with you on the length of sentence, but I am afraid that I cannot agree that it should be suspended". With those words I was condemned to a period of two years imprisonment at one of Her Majesty's establishments. Of course, I soon learnt that this would mean release after one year with a further year "on licence", and even that would be reduced by a further four and a half months providing I satisfied certain conditions such as good behaviour. So, I knew that I had to get through a period of seven and a half months.

The case itself was held at Oakham Castle, which is apparently the longest-running seat of justice in England. The first record of an assize is in 1229 and a crown court is held in the castle every two years; so, every other year Leicester Crown Court decamps to Oakham for this piece of theatre. The courtroom remains in the Great Hall which is decorated by a magnificent collection of two hundred and thirty large horseshoes. The unique tradition is that peers of the realm should forfeit a horseshoe to the Lord of the Manor of Oakham on their first visit to the town. It is thought that this tradition is linked to the de Ferrers' family name; Ferrier was the Norman French name for farrier and the horseshoe has been a symbol of the family since Henry de Ferrers arrived in England in 1066. The horseshoes range from the oldest presented by Edward IV in 1470 to that presented by the Duchess of Cornwall in 2014.

The building is one of the best examples of Norman architecture in England, but frankly I was not over-interested in the horseshoes or the architecture that day.

It was in fact more of a civic gathering than a court of law. The local dignitaries had all arrived for the formal procession into the Courtroom, and were no doubt looking forward to the Reception afterwards. In fact my barrister, who hugely disappointed in the quality of defence, also appeared to be in a hurry to leave as he failed to even make contact with me afterwards – no doubt he was going to the Reception as well. I was very disappointed as I did not expect such a lacklustre address to the Court, and I would have been much better to defend myself. At least all the issues of mitigation that I had previously given to the barrister would have been put before the Court. I met the wrong Judge on the wrong day.

I don't propose to recount the facts of the case or my defence submissions, although I may allude to it on occasions. I had pleaded guilty and I have accepted the Court's jurisdiction and sentence in the administration of justice.

My first reaction was that if I could survive five years at a boarding school then I could also survive a few months away in prison. In fact, I remember Jonathan Aitken writing that the best training for his time in prison was his years at Eton. He thought that the ability to live at close quarters with others, the need to get on with your colleagues, and the focus to keep your head down and just get on with it, were all attributes that living away from home at an earlier age were indicative of the benefits of a boarding school experience.

A prison van, managed by the contract company GeoAmery took me back to the Leicester Crown Court building where I was duly processed, just as I would have been if the case had been held in Leicester. Into another van, and we made the short trip to HMP Leicester Welford Road, the outside of which is seen on regular visits into Leicester, but the inside of which I had only seen many years ago as a BOV (Board of Visitors) prison visitor. When I mentioned this to the Reception Officer he smiled wryly and asked if I noticed any changes. Not yet, I said.

I had brought no clothes or toiletries with me, other than what I was wearing. My barrister thought that a suspended sentence was the likely outcome, and this might have been the case had not the Hearing been transferred at late notice to Oakham and heard before a High Court Judge (Mrs Justice Carr), who in her wisdom had decided otherwise. Although I had of course known that a custodial sentence was always a possibility I chose to live and work for the long period of twenty months from the beginning to the end of the Court process on the basis that a suspended sentence was the likely outcome. I don't regret this, because living with the expectation of prison would have been hard. However, I now knew the outcome and at least this was a weight off my mind.

There was in fact no need to bring one's own clothing, although in the course of time it is much preferable, and much more comfortable, to wear your own clothes and shoes. The prison supplies fleece trousers, tee shirts, warm tops, underwear, and if required socks and shoes. Also freely issued are a toothbrush, toothpaste, shaving razor, soap, and sachets of hair shampoo, together with the necessary bedding of sheets, rug, and pillow.

After more form filling and recording of photo, fingerprints, and other security details, the newly arrived prisoners are directed to the Induction Area.

HMP Leicester

The Induction Area for newly arrived inmates contains about twenty double cells, all on ground level. The length of time in this section is dependent on the rate of new arrivals, and only known at short notice. On average there are about five new arrivals every weekday and sometimes on a Saturday – dependent on Friday night arrests and a Saturday morning Magistrate's Court hearing.

An "Induction Orderly" is on hand to brief the new arrivals with some early advice and to answer questions. Orderlies are trusted prisoners who assist the Prison Officers in the day-to-day management of the various functions to make the prison run smoothly.

Scott

Scott was the Induction Orderly that I met first and he proved to be a valuable source of information and advice. He was at Leicester, having been returned from an open prison, in order to face further charges. Any prisoner on remand is detained in a Local or Category B prison (more details later). He had already been convicted of an £8 millions VAT fraud, and was now facing further charges regarding acting as a company director whilst disqualified. The prosecution were also trying to implicate his wife, and Scott was intent on accepting full responsibility in order to clear her of any liability.

Four months later I was to meet Scott again, but this time when he arrived at Sudbury open prison. He had been convicted of the second charge but had managed to get his wife cleared of any involvement. He had been training as a physiotherapist and when released he intends to move to the Boston area where some work awaits him. Regrettably, however, four days later he disappeared from Sudbury when the prison authorities there had had second thoughts, considered him an escape risk, and returned him to Leicester. I am sure that if Scott is given a chance to demonstrate that he really does intend to stay within the law in the future he will not let us down. You probably think that I must be very gullible, but one thing I have learnt is to tell the difference between those who say that they are going to go straight and those that really mean it. Well, I think that I know the difference – time will tell.

I was shown to my cell in the Induction Unit and was pleased when a few minutes later another person came in whom I recognised. He was the same person that I had been speaking to during the enrolment process forty minutes earlier.

Terry

Terry was my first cellmate in prison and the first person I was able to have a conversation with. I soon realised that he was a regular customer, and he was very helpful in telling me what to expect; it was good to be placed with him as he proved to be a kind and very considerate person. He had been arrested in Loughborough for "begging" and the Magistrates had sentenced him to a short 28 days, meaning that he would be out again very soon in two weeks. I have the feeling that the Magistrates thought they were doing him a favour in giving him the opportunity to detoxify from the drugs and alcohol that he was addicted to. Apparently, he, on one side of the road, and his lady partner, on the other side of the road, had both been arrested for begging; they would do this regularly and when £10 was accumulated they would stop begging and spend the proceeds on more drugs – and after that back to more begging. After one night Terry was removed and taken to the special Detox Unit in Leicester prison but during the short time together we talked about life generally. Apart from his obvious falling on hard times he was, and is, a thoroughly decent person, notwithstanding his repeated sentences for short prison terms. I discovered enough to convince me that prison is not the right place for people like Terry. His dependence on drugs is an illness. Prison will probably remove the availability of drugs for two weeks (although there is certainly no shortage of drugs in prison) but after that he will be back on the streets and no doubt back in prison before long. Detoxification is a process that is likely to take longer than two weeks – but more about drugs later.

For the second and third nights I was alone, so watched a lot of TV; it was another programme of the Strictly Come Dancing season and there was plenty of football to watch. I also began reading Hilary Clinton's book explaining how she lost the election to Donald Trump. I never did finish it; apparently it is the most unfinished book (by those reading it) that has been written in recent years.

After three nights in the Induction Wing I was transferred to a new cell on the Main Wing of the prison, which more closely resembles the traditional prison setting of a central area with cells on either side. HMP Leicester has one such wing, whereas I learnt later that Nottingham has four and some London prisons are even larger. Leicester's capacity is about 400 whereas the largest prisons can accommodate over 1500 people. Built on three levels, the metal railings surround the walkways with a latticed spring grid to prevent prisoners falling to a lower level, although these were frequently used as a trampoline to release pent up frustration (not by me). Imagine the scene in the TV series "Porridge" without Ronnie Barker as Fletcher and the comical prison warder Mr.McKay. Although of course Ronnie Barker himself wasn't present, there was plenty of humour and wit amongst the inmates, a sort of gallows humour. There is a general acceptance that the only route out is to look on the bright side of life and make the most of a bad job. Sometimes of course the ability to do this becomes strained and tempers become frayed in the restricted conditions. I was lucky never to become the target of those unable to control their bad temper and violent behaviour - I did not tempt fate by getting involved. In my new cell I met my next roommate, James.

I had previously met James at the Sunday Chapel service and it was arranged that I move in with him on the second tier. It seemed that a good deal of care was taken to place together prisoners who were likely to be compatible, and I was grateful to the female officer who spoke to James to suggest that I join him.

James

I shared with James for the next eight nights until the time that I left Leicester. James was a forty-year-old from a nearby village to mine in Leicestershire, so he knew several residents of that village that I also knew. He had been involved in a previous fraud, selecting a large company and somehow permeating their accounts department and gaining payments for fictitious invoices. Not surprisingly he had been caught, and sentenced to four years. Released after two years from Sudbury open prison to which he had been transferred after a period in a closed prison, he promised his partner that he was finished with crime. Amazingly, however, he then proceeded to repeat his business model, and was subsequently arrested in front of surprised shoppers in the car park of the Fosse Park shopping centre near Leicester. Being on licence from the previous conviction he was returned to prison immediately as he had broken the main term of his licence, that of staying out of trouble. All this is even more surprising because he was obviously a valued employee of a major civil engineering company. He had been earning £80-100k per year on major contracts such as Crossrail in London and various new bridge building projects elsewhere in the country. When I left him in Leicester he was having problems with his partner, and was awaiting his second trial. He was undecided whether to plead guilty and serve out a reduced sentence (as a result of pleading guilty), or plead not guilty and hope the police evidence was insufficient to prove otherwise.

I define a cell as a room in which you can be locked in and are not able to leave at will. The accommodation at Leicester was definitely in that category. Each cell contained two bunk beds, two chairs in a dilapidated state, a table, two sets of cupboards, a television, and a kettle. At the far end, behind a hanging curtain, were the washbasin and a toilet, conveniently placed below the high window, which served as an effective ventilation unit.

Our cell, Level 2 No.13, was the end one, adjacent to the external wall of the prison building. This probably caused it to be colder than the others, because after a few days during an early winter cold spell, and to some surprise, the authorities installed an electric wall radiator, which proved very useful. Perhaps it was in recognition of me being one of the older inmates.

HMP Leicester is a Category B prison and the local prison to receive those convicted at Leicester. It was opened in 1828 and is a small prison by national standards. It is reputed to have the highest external walls of any prison in England, about thirty feet. Only one person has scaled the wall, and he broke his ankle in the process. The prison is certainly "Victorian" and must be a candidate for closure if ever the prison population can be reduced sufficiently (my proposals to bring this about will come later in the book). The site would certainly make an excellent development project, perhaps for affordable homes.

The prison system has four categories.

Cat A: very high security – a prison within a prison

Cat B: prisons like Leicester which are still highly secure

Cat C: less restrictive than Cat B but still termed as "closed conditions"

Cat D: "open" prisons with considerably more freedom for prisoners to lead normal lives, albeit still within the confines of the establishment

These categories are for those which contain all male inmates. I understand that prisons which hold female prisoners are of just a single category, closed not open.

Within these four categories there are of course significant variations in the quality of building and degrees of comfort. My experience at Leicester seems to have been considerably better than others at some other prisons such as Nottingham and Lincoln. Probably due to the smaller number of inmates, and assisted greatly by the high calibre of staff that I certainly witnessed, HMP Leicester seems not to be one of the alleged flash points within the prison system.

Some prisons are directly managed by the Prison Service; others are contracted out to private enterprise, and probably financed by a Private Finance Initiative (PFI). It would appear, from talking to others, that those privately run establishments are very much more modern in construction and the rooms are fitted with modern appliances, and certainly with more sophisticated security systems. Cells are secured by plastic cards and not by the traditional overweight metal keys.

I do not propose to give a day-to-day account of my life in prison, and have no intention of writing a book in competition to Jeffrey Archer's three volumes of Prison Diaries, which are well worth reading. It would be impossible to write so fluently as him and certainly I cannot command such an audience. His publishers even visited him in prison. Mine is Amazon Self Publish.

During my time inside I did in fact read all three volumes detailing Jeffrey Archer's days at Belmarsh, Wayland, North Sea Camp, and Lincoln prisons – a total time of over two years. From his accounts it would appear that the prison regime has improved during the last sixteen years, with some (only some) of the more unnecessary and petty restrictions discontinued. Certainly, the introduction of better sanitation and TVs in every room (cell) are a distinct improvement.

However, I do propose to write about some of my reflections of my time whilst detained at Her Majesty's pleasure. The eleven days and nights spent in HMP Leicester consisted of sleeping, eating, washing, exercising, writing, reading, and watching the TV. In addition to this, there is what is termed "Association", which is mixing with other prisoners.

As regards sleeping, I can honestly say that I have slept very well in prison with not one "bad night". Not that the mattress and pillows are all that comfortable, but I have experienced more uncomfortable beds in hotels. As at home, I always ensured that I was tired before trying to sleep. Probably the realisation that the concerns of the past two years were over and at least I knew what the immediate future held was a factor. Instead of thinking about what may happen, I was thinking about what will happen and how I could shape it.

The food at Leicester was perfectly edible and satisfactory enough to exist on. Meals at lunchtime and early evening were served from the kitchen server area and taken back to one's cell for consumption. There was usually a choice of about five dishes to choose from and therefore it was possible to select at least one option that would prove palatable. Food from the kitchen could of course be topped up by one's individual purchases from the weekly "Canteen" list, funded by earnings from prison activity or money from one's personal account – funds brought into prison or sent in from outside. The amount allowed to be spent each week is limited in accordance with the prisoner's status – details later.

Normal face washing, shaving, and teeth cleaning were carried out at the washbasin in the cell, but access to the showers was available daily and this was a welcome opportunity to get really clean. The showers themselves were efficient and programmed to deliver water at just the right temperature.

There is of course plenty of time for reading, and the Library at Leicester prison contains a good selection of both fiction and non-fiction books to suit all tastes. Also available from the library is a selection of crosswords, copied from the daily papers.

Very soon after arriving I resolved to do some writing. I had always wanted to write a book, but never very sure about what, so this ambition had usually been reduced to "letters to the editor'. However, as this outlet to my literary urge was now temporarily halted, I decided to write some reflections on prison life generally. Nevertheless, I did not commence putting pen to paper until arrival at Sudbury – perhaps for the very good reason that I did not have any pads of A4 paper until then.

Needless to say the television in prison is a lifesaver. I dread to think what prison life might have been like in earlier decades, before each cell was equipped with a TV and before the installation of flushing toilets. Communal television available to dozens of inmates might have been better than nothing, but the selection of which programme to watch would have been likely geared to the lowest common denominator and Newsnight would probably not have received much support. The important thing is to get a roommate with broadly similar preferences – and I was always lucky in this respect. Sky and BT Sport are of course not available, but the Prison TV Service transmits ten channels, BBC, ITV, and a few film channels – quite enough to satisfy most tastes.

Education is provided to inmates at HMP Leicester in association with Milton Keynes College. In the short time I was there I did not have the opportunity to assess the full scope of the courses available. I only attended once in order to complete the compulsory tests to assess mathematical and English language competence and I am happy to report that I passed with distinction in both subjects.

There was a gym for the keep-fit fanatics, but I preferred my exercise to be the regular daily walking time allowed in the prison yard. Visits to the Chapel were made on both the Sundays I was there, but I will write more on that in a later chapter on the Chaplaincy Teams and religion generally.

Association with other prisoners was available either by

making conversation on the prison balconies inside, or outside in the fresh air whilst walking around the prison yard, inside the high walls and beneath a metal mesh roof obviously designed to protect against any aerial escape attempts. During my time at Leicester I met many interesting characters. Some were hardened criminals; others were weak or ignorant persons who were often the victims of parental failure and the fall-out of alcohol and drug abuse. As compared with Sudbury where the preponderance of fraud and drug trafficking offenders was noticeable, the inmates at Leicester seemed to concentrate on violence (very often domestic violence), burglary, and of course the longer-term inmates in for murder and other heinous crimes. I met one gentleman in prison for murdering his wife and then cutting up her body before wheeling it in a barrow to the refuse dump. He seemed to think it was quite funny.

Whatever the crime, and some are absolutely unspeakably horrible, it is amazing how often the offender appears to be a perfectly reasonable person. I discovered that in nearly every case it was alcohol or drugs that had turned this otherwise normal character into a vicious and dangerous person.

At Leicester, particularly, there was a faction of inmates who are best described as thugs. They are not the type of person one would want to meet on a late-night walk back to the car in the city centre, and even in prison it was sensible to avoid contact with them. They are the ones who make the prison officers' lives more stressful and dangerous, but in the main these officers do a good job in keeping a lid on a potential powder pot. From future conversations with others who had been to elsewhere in the Category B network of prisons I was glad and lucky to be at Leicester.

Chris

Chris was a forty-year-old man from Broughton Astley in Leicestershire. He was in prison for assaulting his wife, although he told me that relationships were now okay and he was looking forward to getting home after a short sentence. He seemed a level-headed person otherwise, but he had "flicked" at the wrong moment and took his frustration out on the person who happened to be standing up to him at the time. I met several similar cases of family violence, some of which had resulted in a death.

Michael

Michael was a thirty-year-old serial burglar. By his own admission he had burgled numerous Leicestershire houses to fund his lifestyle which included the need to purchase drugs. I got the impression that on release he was most likely to return to his chosen career and take the consequences when and if he was caught again. I read in today's newspaper that police expect to solve less than 5% of burglaries, so he can probably have an extended liberty before being caught again.

After a few days I received a note posted under the door. This was to advise me that I was now categorised as a Category D prisoner. This meant that I was considered as "low-risk" – thank goodness for that. Furthermore, I could expect transfer to a Category D prison at Sudbury, which is an open prison for which Leicester is a feeder prison. I was going to spend a few months in Derbyshire – for the second time in my life.

My spell at Leicester Prison is not what I intended, but it was certainly an interesting experience, and one which had begun to stir in me a realisation that the country has some bigger social problems than I thought it had.

My overriding impression of HMP Leicester is that it is an efficiently managed establishment in an outdated Victorian building – but the officers and staff do a good job.

After eleven days at Leicester I duly received a slip informing me that I would be moved to Sudbury the following morning and that I must be ready and packed by 7.30 am.

I was ready for it.

HMP Sudbury

There was no need to encourage me to pack all my belongings in two large plastic bags ready for the Tuesday "ship out". There are no suitcases in prison; everything is packed in large polythene bags and if transported from prison to prison secured by a plastic seal. Eventually called at 10.00 a.m., I was duly processed out of Leicester and boarded a "bus" for Sudbury.

All the travel arrangements and prison movements are contracted out to private enterprise. Clearly there is a large saving to be made as the transport being used is suitable for high security prisoners. For those prisoners being sent to an open low security establishment it makes little sense to use low capacity, high security, and fuel guzzling vehicles. I was told the charge for a one-prisoner movement is £400. If this is the case, it was an early example I encountered of a potential saving. If a prisoner is already established as Category D, and therefore of low or minimal risk, there is little point in transporting him in a state of high security to a fresh establishment that he would be able to walk out of the moment he arrives.

Along with three others, I was driven out of Leicester via Fosse Park, up the M1 motorway, leaving at Junction 24 on the A57 towards Stoke. After about one hour we duly arrived at HMP Sudbury for another processing in. This included a register of all my possessions, a brief health check, and an accommodation interview, which assigned me to a room. I received an ID card - £5 for a new one if lost – and two keys, one for the external door to the accommodation block and the other for my room itself. Good to actually have some keys in my pocket!

A prisoner, another Inductions Orderly, then gave the four men transported from Leicester a brief run-down of the prison timetable and some of the more obvious regulations. Then we put the entire luggage onto a large trolley for the 150 yards walk to Block West 5, which is the first port of call for all new arrivals.

Elliott

Elliott was this Inductions Orderly and the first person I met at Sudbury. His room was also in the New Arrivals Wing so he was on hand to answer any early queries. He was a well-built person, aged about forty, and was serving six years for VAT fraud. There are several inmates at Sudbury for similar offences, which usually involves either fictitious invoices for non-existent purchases, or alternatively a lack of invoices for goods sold – or at least a lack of invoices in the company's accounting records. In the textile trade, where most of my working life was spent, VAT fraud was often committed by invoicing clothing as children's size (VAT 0%) instead of adult's size (VAT 20%); there was plenty of scope for confusion with elasticated fabrics and "one size fits all" garments. It reminded me of a solicitor friend who told me that he once had a Manchester client who had told him that "VAT has not really caught on around here". Elliott obviously knew the whole prison system very well and is in his last year. Latterly he was leaving the prison every weekday for a job outside. As part of the rehabilitation policy, prisoners in their last year, subject to security checks, may be allowed to take employment with a willing employer, and many inmates do in fact leave for work situations in Derby, Uttoxeter, Stoke, and other places every day.

The obvious freedom of movement at Sudbury was immediately apparent, especially in contrast to the confinement at Leicester. Sudbury is an old American Airforce hospital base opened for use after D-Day in 1945. It was converted for use as a prison in 1947. It is spread over an area of several acres; in fact I was told that a walk around the perimeter road was one kilometre in distance – and I walked a few hundred of them. The camp (and that word best describes it) consists of many single storey brick-built units. There are fourteen accommodation units, seven on either side of a main corridor. In addition, a further six blocks have been built on the eastern side of the estate. The total accommodation is 213 single rooms and 175 twin rooms, giving an official maximum capacity of 581 (I make it 563). Single rooms are allocated on the basis of medical need, psychiatric reasons, or those who have qualified by length of time at Sudbury. Personally, I preferred company, including with some who became and will remain good friends.

Other buildings house the administration offices, kitchen, eating block, healthcare, library, chapel, gyms, laundry, reception, and a holding block (for any recalcitrant inmates being returned to a Category B prison), together with units for all the many educational and training facilities on offer.

Although all the doors throughout the whole establishment are locked, and only accessible if unlocked by an officer, each prisoner does have control of his own room. I understand that the Governor recently issued a memo to all the staff reminding them to use the word "room" and not "cell". They are very much rooms with exits freely available at all hours, via the door, or I suppose in the event of a fire, through the ground floor window onto the lawn outside.

So the early freedom is presented as a privilege with trust that needs to be reciprocated. From my observations very few inmates do actually fully reciprocate.

Every person has to spend the first three days going around the various centres of activity for induction talks on what is being offered and what is expected. It was all very reminiscent of arriving at a new school and having to learn the ropes as quickly as possible. At least we did not have to learn the School Song within the first fourteen days.

Sudbury is a "working" prison, which means that all prisoners are expected to take part in full-time work or training. I say full-time, but this actually means two short sessions of 8.30 to 11.30 am and 1.30 to 4.15 pm. However, as a man of retirement age, I was not obliged to conform with this regime, and was quickly told by other over 65s not to allow myself to be pressured into applying or being drafted into any regular job commitment. This was good advice, as although some inmates clearly felt the need and benefit of having a job, there are plenty of alternative ways of occupying the day – like writing a book, teaching mathematics, and learning French.

After the initial period of acclimatization, life at Sudbury soon developed into regular days of maintaining mental and physical condition. Sleeping, as at Leicester, was never a problem. I must agree that it is better to have an en-suite bathroom and toilet, but at least there were no sleepless nights. The twin rooms, which were my only experience, contain two single beds, two chairs, a table, and shelves and cupboards for personal clothes and belongings – and of course the essential

19

television. At the end of each corridor, each of about fifteen rooms, are three separate rooms, one containing toilets, another for showers, and the third for washbasins – all very like school. Opposite these is the "washing-up" room and a cleaning cupboard for mops and buckets.

Not being one who is addicted to weight training or using any of the other gymnasium equipment, I kept fit by taking regular walks, morning, afternoon, or both, weather permitting, around the perimeter road skirting the metal or hedge barrier surrounding the camp. Especially when the sun was shining, this was an enjoyable circuit, completed usually four times per session. It was good to meet other walkers and get to know more about all the familiar faces seen regularly. The more popular circuit was anti-clockwise, but I chose to walk clock-wise, much to the amusement of some. I explained that I saw a lot more people walking my way. The prison is in the countryside, so the transition from late autumn, through winter with the snow and slush, into spring with the daffodils and the awakening floral scene, and latterly with plenty of summer warmth was very interesting for someone who is essentially a "townie".

The library at Sudbury proved a daily routine. Apart from a very good selection of all types of books, fact, fiction, and reference, a range of daily newspapers is available. So I became a regular Times reader, in addition of course to the essential Daily Telegraph which I purchased for myself. Frankly, the library is better than most I have visited outside prison. It also contains about ten computers, which inmates can use and gain access to via their own unique passwords. The Education Department building also offers computers, so there is no shortage of facilities to exploit the advantages of computer usage, albeit that there is of course no Internet connection.

Visiting the Chapel also became a regular habit, both for services, coffee breaks, and to give mathematics lessons – but more about the Chapel, the Chaplaincy teams, and religion generally in a later chapter. Other hours were spent reading, writing, watching TV, and also playing chess, several sets of which can be borrowed from the library. There is also a "snooker hall" containing five tables, but I never did have a game. I prefer my snooker with a glass of wine on a side table, and in any case those from the "traveler" community seemed to monopolise the building – a few of them were very good players indeed.

Welcome changes to this routine are afforded by visits, which are allowed three times per month graduating to four times per month after an initial period. The move to four times per month, together with some other marginal benefits, follows a promotion from "Standard" to "Enhanced" status. This is part of the prison policy of carrot and stick. Behave and you will be promoted. Misbehave and you will be demoted to "Entry" or "Basic" levels with consequent reductions in privileges. This is all very "schoolish", but it works, and is the disciplinary structure that the prison officers need in order to maintain some order.

The facilities at Sudbury are basic but perfectly sufficient to survive in. The freedom to move about is welcome, particularly after only a few days in a closed Category B establishment. Any transgression of the principal rules would result in the offender being transferred out of Sudbury back to a closed prison. These transgressions include the obvious one of leaving the site without authority. It would not be difficult to walk around the gate or skip over the hedge to reach the outside, but I was never tempted to try it. It is amazing, however, how often it does happen; some people are obviously unable to control their emotions and are not intelligent enough to realise the inevitable consequences. I was told of one inmate whose luck was out when he bumped into a prison officer across the bar at the local in Sudbury village. One thing is certain – it is easy to walk out illegally, but impossible to walk back in legally.

Sudbury inmates are either those considered as low risk or those who have been high risk in the past but have now been re-classified as low risk. Despite this, there is a regular flow of absconders. Escaping from Sudbury means walking through the level crossing type gate at the main entrance, or alternatively stepping over a low hedge or walking through one of several gaps in the metal fencing. Just be careful not to get your shoes dirty and make sure that no officers are around at the time.

The number taking advantage of this low security seems to average at least one per week. There are notices around the establishment to advise of the consequences of unauthorised leaving and anyone thinking of this is advised to speak to a Prison Listener first; these Prison Listeners are inmates trained to act as a mentor or counsellor to anyone who needs help. Very often a freshly arrived inmate, after several years of confinement in closed conditions, will decide that he just cannot cope with the newly found freedom and decide that he would be much happier back with his old friends and in the more structured lifestyle. If they ask, these potential absconders are told to give it a week, and they usually settle in within that period. Another reason for absconding is simply to get away from current colleagues; sometimes an inmate will amass a collection of debts or favours owed to others and the easiest method of not paying the debt and avoiding any retaliatory action is to remove oneself before that time. One of the good pieces of advice I received early on was never to borrow anything, which was no problem because I did not have to fund any disallowed habits such as drugs or alcohol.

Having a mobile phone is also a "capital" offence, particularly one with Internet access. There really is no need for a basic mobile because there are an adequate number of landlines throughout the camp, and there would be even more if those which were not in working order were in fact repaired. A seasoned inmate told me that 85% of the prisoners are in possession of a mobile, but I doubt if the proportion is quite as high as that. I never saw one, but I was advised never to accept an offer to use someone else's. The danger is that the mobile owner can identify the number rang, and then threaten the person called with the prisoner's exposure. Similarly, if that mobile is subsequently found and confiscated, the prison authorities would be able to identify the numbers that have been rang from it, thus implicating the prisoner with the use of a mobile – which is strictly forbidden.

However, one of the good things about being in prison is the absence of telephone calls asking if you have been mis-sold PPI insurance. I never had this insurance in any case. I was told by Peter who has lived in Paris, that in France the problem is "twenty times worse".

The third type of offence that will accelerate removal back to closed conditions is being caught with alcohol or drugs. Regular checks are made on suspects, but more about drugs in a later chapter. The urge to obtain alcohol amazed me. On one occasion, admittedly at Christmas time, I witnessed one young man who was very intoxicated. Apparently, a carton of vodka had been thrown into the prison, over a low hedge by a friendly colleague of the inebriate. I have to report that during my whole time in prison I did not touch any alcohol, and furthermore I did not notice the absence of it. I do like a drink, in social quantities of course, but I have proved that I can abstain – particularly if I have to. The abstinence has had one beneficial effect – a reduced beer stomach and a modest reduction in weight.

So life at Sudbury is not hard, except for the obvious loss of liberty. There is no open abuse or disobedience in front of the officers because the inmates have too much to lose. In any case, prisoners are only at Sudbury because they have already been judged as suitable for open conditions, and this means they are non-violent or are towards the end of a sentence. However, it should be recorded that there are clearly people at Sudbury who are not suitable for open conditions because they are not prepared to abide by the prison rules.

Jack

My first room-mate at Sudbury was Jack who was aged about thirty. He originated from North Wales, although he had spent several years in Spain following his University education in England. He was serving sixteen months for fraud that involved improperly accepting payment for supplies that were never delivered. He sold goods on the Internet, pocketed the payments received, but did not have the goods to supply. Easy really – but hardly a game plan likely to have long-term prospects. Jack was about to return to Spain, but decided to spend a last weekend in Wales to say good-bye to friends, and also to his former girlfriend. Unfortunately, the girl friend's father was a local police officer. His daughter told her father that the wanted person was in the village and an arrest was duly effected. Jack is most unlikely to re-offend as he realises his offence was stupid and truly regrets his behaviour. Jack moved after a few days to join a friend that he had met in his previous prison at Liverpool, but I spoke with him every day afterwards on one of my many walks, whilst he was working in the Gardens Department and usually attending to the lawns and flower beds.

Jack was due to leave Sudbury before Christmas on licence, and in accordance with the requirements submitted the address at which he would be resident. Not having any family in the country, he gave the address of a friend. However, this address was found to be unacceptable to the authorities as the occupant had just been sent to prison himself. With no alternative address, Jack was planning to stay at Sudbury for the balance of his term of imprisonment (i.e. half his sentence). He told me that he was planning to return to Spain and that the Probation Service was amenable to this proposal.

No sooner had Jack moved out of the room than my next roommate arrived. As the prison is nearly always approaching capacity there are only a very few occasions when a double room is not fully occupied.

Richard

Richard was an interesting character and very different from Jack who moved to join his friend Josh, whose case history I will recount later. Of all the people I met in prison, Richard is the one whom I would like to help most, as he helped me a lot in guiding me through the early days. Having spent half of the past twenty years in a range of prisons throughout the UK he was an expert in prison life and the ways to live with it. Particularly, he told me that it is not prison etiquette to ask a fellow prisoner what his crime was, only how long he is in for. Enquiries about the nature of the crime should be made with tact and in the course of time, and thereafter I followed his advice. Richard had a good sense of humour and we became strong rivals at chess, playing nearly every day until he left. He also supported Derby County and enjoyed watching the football on TV, and reading my copy of the Daily Telegraph sports section; he also enjoyed doing crosswords. His problems with the law resulted from low-level violence and general unruly behaviour, usually if not always as a result of excess alcohol – hence the large number of shorter sentences. He had been divorced several years ago and had lost contact with his two daughters. Although he had had jobs as a high-altitude pylon worker, in recent years he had been unemployed and was living from house to house. He had intermittent contact with his mother and only seemed to have three close friends, two of them drug addicts and the third an alcoholic. In fact, he told me that were it not for his dog, which he hoped was being cared for by his mother, he would happily stay in prison for another three months by which time the weather would be better and the prospects of getting a job, perhaps in the building trade, would be better. In prison he had a bed, accommodation, food, a TV, shower facilities, laundry, fresh air in the countryside, a library with newspapers, a job (working in the kitchen), and above all companionship.

There is a real problem when life in prison is preferable to life outside, and this case, one of many, has re-confirmed my opinion of what society must do to eradicate homelessness and provide some hope for those with Richard's life prospects. However, I do believe that Richard really wants to "go straight", keep out of trouble, and settle down. He needs accommodation and a job. He was a soldier with the Derbyshire Regiment and has been in contact with SAFA, Help for Heroes, and other Service charities. By the time of his release he had been promised some council accommodation and left prison in good heart, albeit with a certain nervousness about the future. I wish him well and will be in contact with him.

Since Richard left we have corresponded and he is keeping out of trouble. Unfortunately, his dog had been given away, so he just hopes it is now with a good owner. He is still in his council accommodation and getting £258 per week in total benefits. As he would lose some of this if he started a job he needs one that will bring in at least £300 per week in order to make it worthwhile. The purpose of Universal Credit is to make work pay in all circumstances so I only hope that when it is rolled out in the Ilkeston area it does just that. Press reports of its introduction so far are not promising but Esther McVey, the new Minister, is determined to deliver it with a human face and make the policy compassionate as well as effective. (STOP PRESS: As I am taking this book to print the news is that Esther has resigned and is replaced by Amber Rudd). It will save money eventually, but until the change in the benefit culture takes hold, it may well cost more in the short-term. Meanwhile Richard has purchased a chess set and is joining a club.

As a prisoner proceeds through his sentence the relevant dates are marked by ROTLs – Release on Temporary Licence. These can take the form of RDR (Day Release) or ROR (Overnight Release), and these follow on to the HDC or Home Detention Curfew date. The prison guidelines indicate that there is flexibility in the application of these stages as "no two offenders are the same – we are all different". In practice, however, the procedure is very much a box ticking exercise and lacks flexibility. Ministry of Justice instructions seem to be all powerful. I would give individual Governors considerably more authority to exercise some common sense. In particular, it makes sense to give those who are clearly no longer any risk the opportunity for employment outside and home visits of a more frequent and extended nature at a much earlier date than their present authority permits.

I ought to add that for those with a record of any violence there is an extra pre-stage to the above. These are called RAVs or Resettlement Assisted Visits and consist of a visit out of the prison grounds into a neighbouring town with a prison officer on a one to one basis. I am told that this can often mean a cup of coffee in a café or even a visit to a McDonalds. However, I also understand that they are to be discontinued owing to the shortage of staff, and, from what I hear, they are a waste of time.

After a few days on the Induction West 5 Wing we were encouraged (sorry – told) to find other accommodation as West 5 was required for more arrivals. It was suggested to me that someone in West 4 was leaving shortly and that I could join David who had himself left the Induction Wing two days earlier, and whom I got on well with.

David

I therefore shared a room with David for a month until his release. About fifty years of age and hailing from near Milton Keynes, David ran his own business, specializing in recruitment for the energy industry. The recent downturn in the fortunes of the UK oil sector, with the world oil price making North Sea production less profitable, with a serious effect on the level of investment in new production, had depressed income for his business which very much depended on supplying staff for those new projects. David was hoping and expecting that the recent recovery in oil prices would restore demand and resurrect his company's fortunes. When I spoke to him later after his release, that was exactly what was happening. He was serving an eighty-day sentence for drink driving. The offence was a short drive between home and the fish and chip shop but regrettably he was four times over the limit - thank goodness there was no accident or injury. Of course, he realises there is no excuse, albeit that he was under considerable personal pressure at the time. David's time in prison was an absolute waste of time – for himself, the prison service, and the public conscience. A community service order would have been the appropriate punishment, which incidentally was what his barrister had advised as the likely sentence. The Judge however thought otherwise.

Richard (my previous room-mate) was a very good "fixer", and he suggested that when David left I should be joined by Michael, whom Richard had identified as compatible and suitable as the next roommate for myself. Richard was always more concerned with looking after others than looking after his own interests.

Michael

Michael shared a room with me for the bulk of the time at Sudbury, until he was discharged just six weeks before myself. Michael had taken early retirement from British Gas and was enjoying life in Scraptoft, a suburb of Leicester, particularly his favourite pastime of cycling. Unfortunately, whilst driving back from his father's funeral in the north of England he was involved in a fatal crash, and his partner of twenty years was killed; Michael had not had a drink but he did admit to the police that he was tired. That was his mistake because he was subsequently charged with causing death by dangerous driving. Apparently, the Judge was reluctant to sentence Michael to a custodial sentence, but the sentencing guidelines require this in the event of a death. So Michael spent three weeks in the notorious Nottingham prison before arriving at Sudbury. He gained a reputation for always wanting to help others, particularly Pete who was awaiting a cataract operation for both eyes and whose sight was badly impaired. Mandatory custodial sentences for death driving offences are clearly inappropriate; Michael's real punishment was losing his partner, and prison served no purpose whatsoever.

Michael's other main quality was his ability to know the names of everybody, and as a consequence our room became the recipient of everyone else's unwanted supplies. In particular, this meant that we amassed enough to open a grocery store, specializing in packets of biscuits, crisps, and all types of breakfast cereal.

Having seen the Governor of Sudbury at the Remembrance Day Service shortly after I had arrived at his establishment, when he placed a wreath on the War Memorial, I knew what he looked like. So when I saw him again whilst taking a mid-session break near the Education Department helping with mathematics tuition, I recognised him as he approached and I asked him "Are you the Governor" to which he replied in the affirmative. I introduced myself and we had several minutes of conversation. He told me that he had been Governor for four years and asked me what I thought of Sudbury, to which I replied that I did not have any experience with which to compare it but it was much as I thought it might be. He said that he wanted to make some improvements but money was tight, sufficient for running costs but not a lot left for capital improvements. I told him that I was assisting in mentoring some inmates with mathematics, and I was surprised at the extent of innumeracy in the prison. He acknowledged this and said that there was now an "underclass" in the country that had been failed by the education system and by a generation of parents who were unwilling or unable to provide the parental support that is necessary to back up any school education. The challenge now was a fire fighting operation. All we can do in this situation, he said, is to try to ensure that the schools now train a new generation that is reasonably competent in literacy and numeracy.

The Governor might wish that he had more financial muscle to improve the facilities at Sudbury, but that does not excuse poor use of existing resources. There seems to be a chronic inability on the part of the prison management to complete the jobs that have been started, and of poor project management generally. A new carpet was fitted in the staff dining room, but before an overhead plumbing leak had been repaired, which resulted in a damaged new carpet. Old and dilapidated showers throughout the prison were being replaced with new units in refurbished facilities with new tiling. Whilst this work was being carried out on the West 4 dorm (mine) we needed to use the facilities of an adjacent dorm. No problem – but did it have to take ten weeks? There were countless examples of unfinished work, both those being carried out by the prison's Projects department, and also where an outside contractor was being used. One of the problems with the contract company employed by the prison seems to be the reluctance to order the parts required for good maintenance of the estate, even just lamp bulbs or door handles. Clearly this is an example of where outsourcing is not always the best solution for the management of public services. The Governor ought to have full control of his budget.

Another huge waste of funds was apparent when the Visiting Room was re-equipped with new chairs and tables. The old chairs were indeed getting very worn and soiled, and they were not very effective in partitioning the younger prisoners from their amorous female partners. So the prison ordered 100 new chairs and 25 low level coffee tables. I know on good authority, from a senior officer, that the total cost was £40,000 – yes, forty thousand pounds. On the basis that the tables probably cost about £50 each, that means the cost of each chair was an amazing £385. I know something about chairs and their cost, and can be confident that the market value of those chairs is no more than £100 each. The cost of refurbishment should therefore have been no more than £12,000. The problem is that the prison was no doubt obliged to purchase from a supplier on the Ministry of Justice approved list of suppliers, with the result that public funds, and therefore the taxpayer, has been "fleeced".

The conversation with the Governor led to another with one of the mathematics teaching staff. I was acting as a "mentor", someone who assists the tutor with those inmates who are struggling. The role of the mentor is to liaise with staff to identify those learners who would benefit from extra assistance, to build a relationship, to gain mutual respect, to build self-esteem and motivation, and work to guide and teach – but not to do it for them. This particular tutor told me that she preferred to teach adults rather than children. At least most of the adults wanted to learn; in her experience this was not the case with children. I asked her if she agreed that children ought to have to pass a "School Leaving Exam" before being allowed to leave school. This would ensure that thousands of illiterate and innumerate young people would not be cast onto the employment scrapheap. Her response was that "she could not agree more". Another mentor interrupted to say that in some Middle Eastern countries this was already the practice.

Although at Leicester the description of prison officers as "screws" was widespread, at Sudbury I did not hear the term very often. I do not know the proportion of officer to inmates, although one would have thought that this ratio ought to be higher in a Cat B prison than in an open Cat D establishment. However, this was not immediately apparent. Certainly, however, the job expectation is different. At the Cat B prison officers have to take a much more authoritarian attitude and are frequently shouted at, abused, and occasionally physically attacked. At the open prison, the constant threat of a return to closed conditions acts as an effective deterrent to bad behaviour and officers are able to adopt a friendlier and more jovial attitude with the inmates, or at least those that respond appropriately.

As with any group of people, prison officers display a range of ability and temperament. Some officers recognise that prisoners are in fact fellow human beings and they react with consideration, fair treatment, and a pleasing courtesy. Some seem to be blind to any dialogue and a very few get the reputation of being less than helpful, to put it mildly. Thankfully, however the good ones greatly outnumber the others, and I found myself that an increasing number were really friendly and would address me by Christian name.

The proportion of female to male officers who were in direct contact with prisoners was surprisingly higher at Leicester. Perhaps the presence of female officers, provided they work in conjunction with physically stronger male colleagues, provides a calmer and more settling environment in an all-male setting. At Sudbury, the proportion of female to male was lower, although there are of course plenty of females, some quite young, working in the administrative offices, away from the day-to-day life of the prison. Just as inmates do become "institutionalised" after a long period in captivity, then the officers themselves can become institutionalised after a long period of working in the same conditions, albeit that they are on the other side of the divide and are free to go home between their shifts. The job of a prison officer is really a very mundane one – just as it is for the prisoners. Much time is spent sitting or standing in a watching brief, unlocking and locking doors, giving out newspapers, notices, and letters, together with countless other routine and low skill jobs. I was surprised that young women especially really want to work in the prison service as mixing with scores of uncouth and macho men who are liberal in the use of language can sometimes make them uncomfortable – but no doubt they get used to it.

Some of the officers also have a useful role in their capacity as either a Sentence Office (SO) or a Personal Officer (PO) to the inmates. Each prisoner is assigned both an SO and a PO. The Sentence Officer is responsible for representing the prison on all matters relating to the sentence, the terms of imprisonment, day and overnight releases, and final release date together with all the conditions applying to it. The Personal Officer is responsible for the health and well-being of the prisoner himself, which includes such issues as any reports of bullying (which I never witnessed or experienced). My SO appeared to take a healthy disinterest in most issues, and I never met my PO. Otherwise, the system seemed to work.

As Sudbury describes itself as a "working" prison, so it is a regulation that all inmates, except those excused by age (like myself) or infirmity carry out some full-time work. Where this is not a form of education or training, it is by working in one of the several occupations on offer. I say "on offer" because although one can express a preference which is usually acceptable, it is the final decision of the "Work Board" that will determine how every person is assigned. This Work Board meets every Thursday in order to assess the labour required and the labour available and to requisition the workforce accordingly. If only industry could be organised on similar principles – it is in some countries.

One of the more popular work options is in the kitchen. The more obvious reason for this is the proximity to food and the ability to feed oneself additional quantity, if not quality. The work involves preparing and cooking for the 500 plus inmates under the supervision of the prison "chefs". I use the word "chef" with caution. Unfortunately, the budget provision for food does not permit best quality ingredients, but there is a reasonable choice, and no one is going to starve. The kitchen work starts with the washing up of pots and pans, progressing to the preparation of vegetables, filling baguettes with a variety of fillings, and of course cooking, and usually over-cooking, the offerings for the day.

There were six days when I ate very well. I was recommended to enrol in a domestic cooking course, which consisted of one day per week for six weeks, where a group of us were instructed on basic food hygiene, the principles of diet, and most importantly how to cook a range of meals – cakes, desserts, roasts and a selection of other hot dishes. The big advantage was that we had to eat the production. During the course I had an interesting discussion with Mary, one of the instructresses. She was very disparaging about the management of the kitchens. She said that there were many occasions where an item of food was prepared two days earlier than required, then frozen, then defrosted, and cooked on the day of serving. Not only would it be tastier to cook nearer the time of eating, but also the cost of refrigeration would be saved. The ingredients delivered to the main kitchen were exactly the same and from the same supplier as those delivered to the "Secret Diner" which is a popular café situated just outside the prison gates and run by prison staff and inmates, and open to the public. This outlet served good and popular food, so there was no excuse for a poor offering or bad cooking practice, and she instanced the heating and cooling of curry as a major health risk; apparently curry is one of the worst foods to re-heat. No problem for me – I can't stand it. She would love the opportunity to take control of the main prison kitchen and bring about a much-improved service, and with the same budgetary constraints as at present. I will tell the Governor about this. Nobody expects prison food to be better than that typically consumed outside by the law-abiding population, but there is no reason why it has to be so much worse that it need be.

Strangely, the cooking courses were not over-subscribed, and I soon realised why. A large proportion, and certainly a majority, of the inmate population are non-white and therefore do not like typical English dishes such as fish pie, shepherd's pie and apple crumble, all the dishes we learnt on the course. In fact, the Asian and Afro-Caribbean ethnic men do a lot of "home cooking" – that is preparing their own food in the kitchenette at the end of each corridor with food purchased in the weekly prison shop. Personally, I would like to have done the course again, and again – but once is the limit.

Another large group of inmates are employed in the Gardening Department. At Leicester, of course, this was not an option, but at Sudbury it is necessary to maintain a large area, most of which is grass and soil. Grass mowing, weeding, digging, sweeping are all the regular jobs, and there is a continuing programme of improvement by planting new bulbs and bringing uncultivated areas into order. Trusted prisoners were responsible for a range of equipment, from motor mowers to large earth moving plant. As the spring and summer seasons arrived it was apparent that Sudbury could be quite an attractive setting. On sunny days the heavily tattooed population are to be seen reclining and relaxing on the lawns on both sides of the estate, absorbing the sun's rays probably to a harmful extent. What the place really needs is an open-air swimming pool. Certainly, the army of gardeners do a good job. More accurately, a few of them do a good job and are obviously experienced; many others treat the occupation as a means of doing very little whilst still enjoying the fresh air. Not surprisingly, there are many men who are intending to become gardeners and landscapers when they are released. The job is good for those who wish to be self-employed, are prepared to work hard, and have no other obvious trade to work in.

The Textile Workshop did have a contract with a well-known national store chain to receive all the customer returns, remove the store identification, leave the fibre content and washing instructions of course, and fold, prepare, and pack for onward sale to Africa – or some other willing buyer. I am told that there were problems when several of the "workers" in that building were seen wearing very good quality brand new garments, but this was probably not the reason for the contract not being renewed. Whatever would St. Michael have thought? Other similar work is now carried out in that department, but the work is low skill and is really the equivalent of the image of prisoners mending mailbags in the folklore of prison history. I did in fact offer to go to London and negotiate some new contracts with other retailers, but this was not taken up.

Another work department was called Recycling. This includes the receipt of obsolescent electrical equipment, mainly old televisions, dismantling these into the constituent parts – wires, screens, frames, plugs, etc. – and dispatching to onward addresses that no doubt complete the recycling process.

About two dozen inmates were employed in the Fence Panelling department, and I got to know several of these well. The work involved the construction of garden fence panels, and consisted of nailing the horizontal boards to the vertical frame with the use of nail guns, very dangerous instruments in the wrong hands, to produce what looks like the average garden fence panel that is on sale in countless garden centres and builders' yards. The raw wood is delivered by the client customer already cut to size and shape, and the finished production, neatly stacked on pallets, is collected periodically. Unfortunately, however, the quality of production management is such that there are frequent stoppages due to the lack of raw material or quality control issues. This is a pity, because it is clearly one operation from which the prison should be able to make a worthwhile commercial surplus. No doubt the fence panel outlet gets its product at a very competitive price as the cost of labour at £10 per WEEK is slightly higher than that of slave labour. In fairness, a production bonus of an extra £20 per week is paid if output reaches a certain level, but is rarely achieved because of the stoppages.

In this department there are about ten teams, each of two men working in pairs, which assemble the panels. The method of working varies wildly as there is no effective instruction given other than a brief initial demonstration. Consequently, the output of each team varies considerably, together with variations in quality, which would be unacceptable in normal industry. Additionally, whereas some teams work conscientiously, others resent being told to do any work at all.

It is quite apparent that this department is employing at least double the number required to satisfy the fence panel company's production requirement. Any policy to maximise prison income from external sources would include reducing the fence panel workforce to five or six teams, with effective management to eliminate the shortage problems and incentivise the men. Meanwhile, the remaining men could be deployed on another production line manufacturing another product for another customer. A much greater emphasis on the productive potential of the prison population should be encouraged in order to generate additional finance to fund prison improvements. Here again, one suspects that the dead hand of the Ministry of Justice and the Prison Department is stifling any entrepreneurial spirit that might just exist in the Governor and his staff.

Carpentry is another work department. This involves the production of wood cut to many required shapes and sizes on what looks like some very sophisticated and expensive machinery. The end products are tables and similar articles. It has to be said, however, that this large area was usually a hive of inactivity.

Products is the title of the last money-making department, or in this case usually money saving. The unit employs inmates who have a skill that can be used in the maintenance of the Sudbury estate itself. There is a constant and on-going requirement for electrical, woodworking, and plumbing repairs and maintenance work, and any opportunity to avoid calling in outside contractors to do this work is obviously very welcome.

We thought that it was an indication of a pro-active listening prison management when some of us were selected as representatives of the over 55 age group. One of the Deputy Governors was calling a meeting to discuss ways in which the prison could better cater for the more senior (in age) of us. Unfortunately, the meeting was cancelled at late notice and no reason was given. We were assured that it would be rearranged for another day, but this never happened, at least before I left, but if the meeting had taken place there were a number of issues that would have been raised. Better kitchen management even with the same financial constraints would considerably improve the tastiness and nutritional value of the daily food offerings. Better management of the prison workforce would significantly improve the standards of hygiene, emptying of dustbins, removal of mould, prompt repair of malfunctioning equipment, and completion of minor works. However, we would have thanked the management for keeping the radiators on full-time during an especially cold spell – that was very considerate.

The other main topic of debate would have been the allocation of rooms. One school of thought would see all the older inmates segregated into reserved wings, away from the younger more rowdy ones. Another group, myself included, preferred the current system that leaves inmates to organise themselves (subject to any security concerns the officers might have). One benefit of this is that there is a mix of age groups within each wing, and it could be argued that the older ones exerted a calming influence on the younger ones. The other issue was of course greater flexibility for permitting temporary releases for those who might have an infirm wife or other pressing domestic requirement.

So life at Sudbury passed by, week by week, month by month. The so-called "beast from the east" brought some icily cold weather and snow. That was the outside; inside the radiators were running at full capacity. Michael was approaching his discharge date and introducing me to some of his work colleagues who were fine-tuning their own plans for life after release. Getting work for an ex-prisoner is of course more difficult than for someone with a clean record. There are some good examples of major employers who specifically set out to employ ex-prisoners – Timpson's, the shoe repairer and key cutter, is a good example – but very often a prisoner will choose to opt for self-employment particularly if he has a skill which is in demand. I was pleased to be able to help about six fellow inmates with the preparation of their Business Plans, which were aimed at firstly proving the viability of the project to the person himself, and secondly convincing any potential funder to support the new business. There is in fact a lot of business and commercial support available to ex-prisoners who are starting up on their own, and there are several charitable and grant making bodies that are prepared to give grants or modest loans for good start-up proposals. They all require a well prepared and reasoned Business Plan.

As the cold weather spell concluded we were then thrust into an early summer and some very hot weather. The rooms themselves were well insulated and not unpleasantly stifling. Outside, there were examples of all shapes and sizes in varying degrees of undress. Walking around the grounds in a topless state was not allowed but sunbathing on the lawns was commonplace. Wearing my sunhat I must have looked like some English explorer in Africa because I attracted the title of Dr Livingstone. I was rather pleased that so many of the inmates had even heard of Dr Livingstone, I presume.

One of the regular jobs that I did commit to was collecting the morning papers every day from the Gate and bringing them back to the Central Office where they could be collected by those who had ordered their own newspaper. I first offered to do this because it was the best way of getting the papers at breakfast time rather that later in the morning when one of the officers had bothered to collect them. It became my job and I was known as the oldest paperboy in the country. On weekdays there were only a few papers to collect – one Financial Times, a Times, my Telegraph, a Daily Mail and about three Suns. On Saturdays and Sundays the volume increased substantially and the proportion of Suns and Daily Mirrors was high. I say with confidence that there will never be such an efficient paperboy at Sudbury again.

The Healthcare at Sudbury is certainly free at the point of use. In fact it is micro-managed for each one of the prison population. Every day a long list of appointments is posted at various vantage points throughout the campus, some of them requested by the prisoner and others as part of the comprehensive screening process; failure to attend an appointment is registered on one's disciplinary record. Until one is assessed as responsible and capable of looking after one's own medication there is a queue every morning and afternoon to collect the prescribed dose of tablets. It is all very regimented, but it obviously needs to be in the case of many of the inmates. Apart from treatment for all the usual aches, pains, and sicknesses there is facility for dental care and also a visiting optician. On a regular diabetes check-up I was summoned to see a podiatrician (yes, I have checked the spelling) for the usual inspection to ensure that the soles of one's feet are sensitive to pinpricks. I passed the tests and then the young lady doing this work asked me if I would like her to give me a full pedicure and remove any rough skin. I have to say that my feet felt really good after this visit, and I had a repeat visit for the same treatment shortly before discharge. I told the young lady that she could earn at least £40 for doing that outside – I think she knew it already.

If there is any treatment that cannot be carried out in the Healthcare Unit there is a regular stream of patients taxied over to Derby or Burton on Trent Hospital (escorted by an officer of course), in order to receive specialist care including operations on eyes (cataracts), broken bones, hip or knee operations, and an ambulance is summoned for the occasional heart attack. So, in summary, I have to complement the prison service for the medical care of its temporary customers. In fact, if you do have an illness, you might well be better cared for in prison than outside – providing of course you don't catch one of the bugs that are prevalent in any confined space, be it a school or prison or even hospital.

The Healthcare doctors are very aware that prisons generally are susceptible to contagious infections. Well, there is plenty of fresh air and opportunity to keep fit, but hygiene could and should be improved by more attention to waste disposal and standards of sanitation. In general, the prisoners make the best of a bad job. At least there was no excuse for less than clean clothes and bed linen. The laundry service, operated of course by prisoners working in the small building near the library, contained five industrial washing machines and five industrial spin dryers, so one's laundry contained in a string laundry bag could be taken in the morning and collected in the evening on the prescribed day of the week. Likewise, the Central Stores would replace sheets, pillowcases, and all prison clothing (if you used it) as required.

The day arrived for my roommate of four months to be himself discharged. Michael was ready for this and looking forward to seeing his beloved Yorkshire again (albeit that his current address is in Leicestershire). He was also very eager to make sure that he was replaced by someone compatible for me. Aware of his impending departure I had, however, been looking out for just such a person – someone who liked politics and current affairs TV programmes, liked Mozart, Beethoven, Bach, and Handel, and who was generally an educated, courteous, and considerate man. I was lucky.

Peter

Peter arrived at Sudbury after a year in a Cat C prison in the south of England, and he was certainly the most qualified academically person that I met whilst in prison – and probably before and afterwards as well. His first impression of Sudbury was of amazing freedom but he soon acclimatised himself into a daily routine of prison life which often included twenty laps of walking around the estate. He told me that he had been involved with fraudulently registering inaccurate data in connection with work at his previous University. That was fifteen years ago, and after teaching modern languages at a few schools in the home counties he duly moved to another post in Paris, a city where he still maintains his apartment. On a return visit to England he was arrested, charged, prosecuted, and duly sentenced to five years imprisonment for offences relating to the misrepresentation of his cv following the earlier incident. There was pecuniary advantage to himself but certainly no financial loss to any organisation, and domestic pressures were certainly a contributory factor. This all sounded rather harsh to me, without of course then knowing the full facts of the case. I now know the full facts and still think his custodial sentence was extremely harsh, and unnecessary. His offences were certainly illegal, but they were not sinful. I became very friendly with Peter as he was clearly not the typical Sudbury inhabitant. He spoke six languages, English, French, German, Italian, Spanish, and Hungarian, together with a less fluent knowledge of others. His speciality was that of English and French literature; he had also written a treatise on Mozart and his Masonic music.

Early on Peter said that he would like to do some teaching of a foreign language to a small group of fellow inmates who would like to learn one. After some consideration, we decided on French, and I looked forward to the twice-weekly sessions arranged for Wednesday evening and Sunday afternoons. He assured me that before I left Sudbury I would be able to understand French, even if not fluent to speak it.

Ma pire matière à l'école était le français. Sans les vacances je n'ai jamais parlé le français, et même en vacances c'était seulement pour commander une bière ou un verre de vin. Donc quand Pierre est arrivé à Sudbury janvrier et quelques-uns de nous ont compris qu'il a parlé six langues aisement, et il nous a offert à apprendre, j'ai décidé qu'il serait une bonné idée à passer le temps et mieux encore pour garder l'esprit actif. Mes trois activités d'apprendre le français, à enseigner les mathmétiques à pleusieurs des prisoniers, et aussi d'écrire ce livre ont rempli mes jours jusqu' à le temps quand je serai libéré.

Nous nous sommes rencontrés deux fois chaque semaine pour les conversations dans la sale à manger, mercredi et dimanche. Pierre aussi m'a donné des leçons supplémentaires, particulièrement quand nous avons partagé une salle plus tard. Il a concentré sur la grammaire et la construction des phrases. Maintenant je dois concentrer le vocabulaire et le genre de chaque nom. Vous remarquerez la resemblance entre pleusieurs mots français et anglais.

Je continuerai à écrire et apprendre Pierre, donc j'espère que mon français s'améliorera à l'avenir. Je travaillerai chez moi, et je pense qu'un vacance en France sera necessaire.

(Translations are available on request)

So, in addition to considerably improving my French, I also enjoyed his love of music, particularly Beethoven. There was only one area of disagreement – Brexit – but as he had come from France his views were not unexpected. We agreed to disagree.

Eventually, my turn to leave approached. On the eve of departure I went round thanking some of the staff for their kindnesses and to as many fellow inmates as I could identify with to wish them all the best for the future. It had been a truly life changing experience to meet so many different characters, some bad, but some very good people indeed.

God bless them all.

Offences and Offenders

I have tried to analyse the different categories of offences that I have come into contact with, and also the different types of offenders that committed them. It must, however, be recorded that there are two classes of offenders that I have not met and the first of these is terrorists. A few years ago this category principally consisted of IRA murderers and bombers, but nowadays the usual source emanates from Islamic fundamentalism. These prisoners are held in specific prisons and do not mix with those I have had the experience of meeting. The other category that I have no experience of is that of sex offenders who are also congregated in a limited number of establishments, or at least in separate holding areas of the regional and local prison network. There is still in prison a distinct perception of what is right and what is wrong, and the nature of which offences are "less bad" than others, and sex offenders are not generally held in good light in that context.

By far the largest category of inmates was for drug related offences in one form or another. This includes those convicted of supplying or possessing, and also committing other crimes for the purpose of funding the consumption of drugs. It was a category that I was particularly eager to learn more about, and I have devoted a later chapter in this book to the subject of drugs – including my proposals for dealing with the problem. Some of the case histories of those I have interviewed have therefore been included in that chapter.

In this book I have interspersed my reflections with the stories of many of the interesting people that I have met whilst in prison. There were of course dozens of others that I spoke to, and towards the end I would frequently be hailed by "John, I want to be in your book". However, in fairness to everyone and so that I was able to assure everyone of anonymity, the Christian names of the characters recorded in this book have been changed, and I have omitted surnames completely. In truth, I knew very few surnames, as prison is very much a place where only Christian or nicknames are used. As the introduction to the old TV crime series "Dragnet" went – "The names have been changed to protect the innocent" - in this book, the guilty as well.

It should be said at this point that at both Leicester and Sudbury at least 50% of the inmates are innocent of the offence for which they have been convicted. I have to report that this is what they told me, and I felt absolutely no inclination to doubt this, suggest otherwise, even less to actually disagree with them. Several of the men were not even present at the scene of the crime. The police and CPS somehow prosecuted the wrong person. In two cases the Judge was clearly corrupt and the whole British judicial system has been brought into disrepute. In many cases the police simply "had it in for me". I have retold all the case histories as told to me. I soon learnt not to believe all I was told, or at lease to strongly suspect that I was not being told the whole story.

The length of sentence quoted in any of the case histories I relate were those imposed by the Court. For sentences less than four years it is usual that half is served in custody and the balance is served on licence, released but monitored by the Probation Service. Some years ago, in an effort to reduce the prison population, the first part of any sentence up to four years was further shortened by allowing prisoners release on temporary licence, permitted to go home or some other approved address, but subject to some curfew restrictions. In this way the custodial portion of a sentence can be reduced by a further four and a half months. This earlier release is not an entitlement, but is at the discretion of the prison authorities. In fact, the prison management is sometimes unfortunately looking for an excuse not to permit it. In one case, Fred was serving a short sentence for failing to register for VAT after his business had exceeded the threshold of £85k for registration. He had traded for two years expanding the business to sales of about £240k and consequently had defrauded HMRC of VAT income over a two-year period. I didn't think that prison was the most suitable form of punishment for his offence, but was even more surprised when he was refused the early release on licence because thirty years ago he had pleaded guilty to renting a small property for the purposes of immoral activity, prostitution. Fred's solicitor was appealing the decision, but, as is often the case, by the time the appeal would have been heard it was the date for release in any case.

At the time of writing, reports of the CPS/Police withholding vital evidence from defence counsels is in the news. These pieces of evidence are often mobile telephone or text messages that would have reinforced the defence case, but have been mislaid or conveniently ignored either by negligence, genuine error, or perhaps worse. These have resulted in several cases being dropped and many more being reviewed, a number which presently amounts to several hundred or more. So one can never be absolutely sure that some of the claims of miscarriage of justice do not have some validity. In fact, it is certain that there are some innocent people in prison. It is better that one guilty person goes free than one innocent person is imprisoned – Discuss. It does remind us, however, never to completely dismiss a claim of innocence.

There were two features common to the vast majority of inmates. One was body tattoos. The other was the vocabulary – almost every sentence contains at least two words both beginning with the letter "f". Another observation is the fraternal nature of life in prison. Everyone, or at least the large majority, realises that the best way of "getting through it" is to be supportive of others. The shared challenge of surviving the loss of liberty and living out the sentence imposed by the Court leads to a remarkable spirit of comradeship. "After you", "All right mate", "Are you ok" are heard with frequency. Although the prison is full of convicted inmates, some for the most heinous of crimes, it is still true to say that there is a camaraderie and brotherhood that is not always apparent in the outside world.

One amusing altercation I overheard was an exchange between two men, one of whom had obviously been accused of pilfering something. "I am not a thief you know; I am a murderer". That rather sums up the antagonism of prisoners to the act of theft – or at least if from a fellow prisoner. Having said that, it was still an early piece of advice to make sure your room was always left locked, and double locked if out for more than a few minutes. The prison is not lacking in people who are very capable of opening a lock with just a piece of metal or plastic.

Josh

Josh came from the south coast, although he had spent some time in Liverpool prior to arriving at Sudbury. He was definitely intending to return to crime on release, as he doesn't know anything else that would generate sufficient income to live on. However, next time he won't hang around long enough to be detected – he will disappear to the Costa del Crime or a similar sunny climate. His crime was one that sickened me. He had defrauded an elderly couple of their £80k life savings by selling them false life insurance. I know it seems incredible that anyone could be persuaded to part with £80k, albeit in about six tranches, but if you have a sophisticated telemarketing operation there will always be someone who falls for a scam of this type – and of course it is the older and more vulnerable ones who are targeted. Josh thought the whole episode was funny and with his training at the Sudbury University of Crime he is dreaming up future business plans for when he is released. Beware. Later on I asked Josh if he was still planning to do similar scams. "Yes" he said, and then on reflection, "but I wish I could target a bank rather than an old couple"

Chris

Chris had received a five-year sentence for gun crime. Apparently he had owned a rifle without the required licence. I was assured that this was only in the capacity of a collector of such firearms for historical purposes and that it had never been used in anger. However, unfortunately, during a demonstration to friends, the gun had gone off and a police enquiry resulted following a neighbour's reporting of a loud noise. Chris' case was not helped when the Police discovered some drugs at his house during their investigation, although they were assured the drugs were for personal use only. Gun

50

crime seems to be one class of offence that the Courts regard with great seriousness. I am not arguing against this because no one wants the UK to be like the USA where the ownership of firearms is of course prevalent and where regular shooting outrages are the subject of our news. At the time of writing news has just arrived of another school shooting, this time killing nineteen children and teachers in their Florida school, by a former pupil taking revenge for having been excluded. This was the nineteenth such incident so far this year, in just two months, and these statistics will be out of date by the time you read this.

Chris is truly repentant for his offence. He was a shy person, but someone with a heart of gold. He was one of the "Chapel Orderlies", making arrangements for the different activities held in the Chapel, keeping the place clean and tidy, and addressing all the newcomers at their Induction Meeting about the facilities available for private meditation and pastoral support. During the Christmas period, when the place was seasonally busy, Chris did a great job in dealing with the higher volume of callers than normal. He would give emotional support to many, often with a cup of tea and a biscuit. He was almost an additional member of the Pastoral Team.

Chris came from Guildford and received visits from his wife and three sons. He was very keen to improve himself and make good some of his educational shortcomings. Before his offence he had worked as a Bouncer at a local pub, but on release he wants to take up other opportunities. There is no further public benefit in his continued imprisonment.

Basil

Basil, or Bas as he introduced himself to me when we met on a walk, told me that he was in prison for armed robbery and, sentenced to twelve years, he was at Sudbury for the last year of his incarceration. He told me that he was the owner of a small/medium size construction company in the north of England which was being run by his two sons during his temporary absence. His advice to me was not to rely on anyone else and to stay completely independent. He himself was definitely a "loner", deciding not to do any work, as was his entitlement as an over-65. Being determined to keep fit, he would walk several laps of the prison every morning, and as I would walk in the opposite direction I saw him fairly frequently. Bas complained that he himself was never actually involved in the armed robbery – it was his brother. Coming to the end of his sentence, he was very upset that the police were still investigating him in respect of other offences. Time will tell; the law moves very slowly.

Shokut

Shokut was someone who asked for my help in reading his letters with the objective of improving the English and particularly correcting any grammatical mistakes – of which there were many. These letters, to either his legal advisers or directly to the Judge who had sentenced him, were generally long works of twenty pages or more. They were full of accusations of corruption and dereliction of duty by the Judge and malpractice by the police officers who had investigated the offence. He told me that one police officer had been dismissed and two others had taken early retirement as a result of an enquiry relating to his case, but I am not certain this is the whole truth.

Shokut's offence was one of mortgage fraud. His mortgage broker, who had somehow managed to absolve himself of all responsibility, had secured funds for the purchase of properties in the Birmingham area by giving inaccurate levels of income. There did not appear to be any financial loss as all the mortgages obtained had been serviced and were fully paid up to date, and the mortgage companies themselves were not parties to the complaints. It transpired that the Police motive in pursuing Shokut was probably the likely fact that the funding to commence this programme of property investment had allegedly been sourced from the proceeds of drugs trading. Family members had reputedly been involved in this activity and had been convicted in some seriously large cases of drugs importation. Shokut was approaching the time when he was to be released on parole, but was now facing a POCA (Proceeds of Crime Act) claim for £4 millions. This was significantly more than the total value of his remaining portfolio of properties, even before mortgage debts were taken into consideration, so the claim must have included other sums about which I was not told. However, it appears that the total proceeds of crime are calculated by including all the rents that he had received for the past ten to fifteen years, with no allowance for any expenses. As any Buy to Let investor will know, the cost of mortgage interest, repairs and maintenance, insurance, and administrative costs absorb a large proportion of any rental income received. The full claim, excluding these costs, seems high to say the least.

I told Shokut that I was happy to review his letters, but only to correct the grammar; I was not competent to advise on legal matters. However, I did advise him that it was probably not a good idea to accuse the Judge of corruption and abuse of position, and advised him to take further legal advice before sending any more letters directly to the Court, and that it would probably be a worthwhile strategy to sell some of his properties in order to be in a position to make a sensible offer of settlement of the POCA claim.

On the day of his release Shokut came to see me, to thank me for all my work, and give me his calculator as a thank-you present. He often asked for my contact details, which I was careful to avoid giving him.

Ray

Ray, a native of one of Leicestershire's market towns, was serving a thirty months sentence for VAT fraud. He told me that the VAT errors on his quarterly returns were actually made by two of his bookkeepers, but as a director of the company he himself had been prosecuted. Ray was one of several in Sudbury for fraud associated with VAT. I would have thought a stern financial penalty was more appropriate for this type of offence, particularly a first offence.

Mark

Mark was a golf professional, and in fact intends to be one again after his release. He received a sentence of one year for an involvement in a fraud concerning his golf club. He had been sponsored by a company of which his lady partner (not his wife) was in control. Unfortunately, the amount that the company should have paid the golf club for this sponsorship was not the same as that which was received by the club. The balance had been paid directly to Mark. One would have thought that the responsible person was Mark's lady friend. However, the evidence of her and her son convinced the Court that Mark was the culprit. Are you as confused as I am? Perhaps this was another case where I have not been told the whole truth, and nothing but the truth. On further reflection, I have probably not been told any of the truth.

Peter

Peter was from Leicester and arrived at Leicester exactly one week after myself. I remember seeing pictures of him on the local TV news. He had been accused of selling motor vehicles, which were un-roadworthy, to members of the general public, and it was alleged he had been threatening to those who had complained and wanted to return their purchase. The case had been brought by the Trading Standards Department for which he had received a sentence of three and a half years. On the TV and in the press Peter was painted as a thoroughly undesirable and offensive bully. He was transported out of HMP Leicester only three days after arrival – a very short period of time. The reason was soon apparent – a female prison officer at Leicester had recognised Peter on arrival and immediately reported to her superiors that she and Peter had had a romantic association in the past. That might otherwise have made for some interesting observations. However, Peter was shipped to Sudbury on the same day as myself and I got to know him there over several months. All I can say is that I found him to be a decent and likeable person, quite unlike the ogre depicted by the media and obviously presumed by the Judge. There is no doubt that he was selling un-roadworthy vehicles, but I have difficulty in believing that the Court could not think of a better punishment for Peter than the custodial sentence he received, which was in addition to a much longer ban in any work connected with the motor industry.

John

John was an interesting character. When asked what crime he had committed to deserve a six-year sentence, his reply was "Revenge". I was aware that this was against the Ten Commandments, but not part of the UK criminal code, or at least unless translated into further action. The full facts eventually surfaced. As a self-employed tradesman, he was owed £400 by a customer who was refusing to pay him.

Instead of pursuing this debt through the normal channels John had kidnapped his customer and kept him tethered to a chair for a whole week. I don't know if he ever got his money, but he has certainly had time to reflect on his actions. John spent his time at Sudbury in self-education and he was hoping to arrange some external coursework at Trent University when he reaches the stage in his sentence to be allowed out. John was a disturbed character, but I am sure that there is no prospect of him re-offending. This is a case where much more flexibility in the conditions for early release would be appropriate. There would be one less person requiring full board at public expense and one more person earning a living and making a contribution to society.

Sulta

Sulta, aged 25, came from Leicester. He had previously been employed at Asda and also at McDonalds in Fosse Park so I was familiar with the locality in which he had worked. He is into the second year of a 58-month sentence (29 to serve) for burglary. He was still very uptight about his conviction, claiming that the amount in question was just £50 and that he had been stitched up by his brother-in-law. There was not a lot of help that I could offer him. I am afraid that this case exhibited the mental anguish and depression that can result if the prisoner is unable to absorb the reality of his situation and concentrate on the future rather than the past – which really is now the past and there is not a lot you can do about it.

Sam

Sam saw me having a walk one day and told me that he was surprised to see me. It transpired, when I asked why, that he was a former pupil at Leicester Grammar School where I was a Founder Governor. Unfortunately, he had become involved with a fraud involving the NHS and his local hospital. He knows that he made big mistakes and only looks forward to the opportunity to re-start his life, although he knows this is unlikely to be with the NHS. His punishment is really the loss of his earlier career prospects. The latest report is that the medical authorities are demonstrating a very forgiving and reasonable attitude.

John

John hailed from Ireland and told me that he had been in prisons in the USA, Mexico, and the UK. John is now serving a five-and-a-half-year sentence for smuggling rhino tusks, and this followed a similar sentence for smuggling cigarettes into the country – duty free of course. He is facing a £2.5 million claim under POCA (Proceeds of Crime Act) and when released before too long he also faces further investigations into another alleged smuggling offence. It doesn't seem to worry him. He has not been assisted in his defences by associations with some well-known (to the police anyway) major drug barons, and also past flirtations with the IRA and its criminal element. Apart from all this he was a very good conversationalist and was a popular person at Sudbury. He also had a big sympathy vote as he now needs the assistance of a wheelchair and crutches. He had just been to Derby Hospital for an operation for one hip replacement and is awaiting a date for the other. He was a regular at all Chapel occasions, and although a Roman Catholic he also received communion at the C of E Service. When finally released he intends to return to his beloved Ireland, where he told me that he is well known for all the wrong reasons. He told me that he still did not really accept that his smuggling was criminal – it might have been illegal but he was actually only satisfying a demand. He told me that he had now "retired" from his job as a professional criminal.

Hardeep

Hardeep comes from Solihull. He is completing a sentence of fourteen months for conspiracy to burglary, accepting goods, which turned out to be stolen. He says that he did not know the goods were stolen, but he did suspect their origin as the price was "very competitive". He runs two businesses, an off-licence and a building and BTL property business. At present he has nearly twenty properties and intends to expand this portfolio on release. He regrets wasting £14k on barrister fees – I particularly sympathised with him on that point. Hardeep is a young man and is clearly going to be successful – providing he stays clear of crime, and I am confident that he will. Before prison he said that he had made business his first priority, and his wife the second priority. From now on his priorities would be reversed. I told him that the same would apply to me as well.

Jay

Jay lives in Aston, near the Villa ground. He is serving six years for possession of a firearm. No use of any firearm was involved and he says that he was not aware of the licence requirements. Ignorance of the law is no excuse, but the sentence does appear harsh. Have I been told the full story? Probably not.

Landhu

Landhu was a Sikh and aged about 60. He was at Leicester Prison when I arrived and we travelled together on the same bus to Sudbury. I met him frequently during our many perambulations and would stop for a chat about Leicester or the textile industry. He was another serving time, two and a half years, for VAT fraud, supplying adult's garments (VAT 20%) and invoicing as children's knitwear (VAT 0%). He had a garment-making factory in Leicester employing about 30 people, and unfortunately his absence from the business was now causing problems. Customers were delaying payments in his absence and his sons and wife, who were continuing to run the firm, were finding it difficult to keep things going. The business was now losing money and Landhu was seeking advice. I told him what the options were. Fortunately, a separate company owned the main asset of the property itself, so the run-down and closure of the manufacturing company could be managed before debts got higher.

Pedro

Pedro was another very interesting character. He is (or probably "was" by now) a Chartered Accountant, in prison for fraud. I was never actually able to learn the full details of the case, but clearly he was able to provide for himself and family in some luxury prior to his arrest. He appeared to treat the justice authorities with a degree of contempt, and was smug that he had relieved his client of a considerable sum which was probably now beyond recovery. Pedro was also a first-class musician, and he demonstrated his proficiency on both the violin and keyboard. His violin, which had recently been delivered to Sudbury, was clearly not an inexpensive one.

Richard

Richard lived locally and was serving a five-and-a-half-year sentence for fraud by deception. He was a minor player in a large scam to sell time-shares which did not exist. He had a speech impediment, but that did not affect his ability and willingness to act as a PID Orderly. PID stands for Prisoner

Information Desk, and his function was to advise on all sorts of enquiries and to provide the multitude of different forms (called Applications) required for just about every request. This is all part of the highly systematic and tick-boxing regime for the management of Sudbury. Richard was previously a multi-lingual sales executive with a large midlands engineering company, and he has plans to start a new business with a friend when he is released. With a year before his planned release Richard is now travelling to Derby every day in order to work at a travel agency business. From all accounts this is a well-paid position, but his salary is paid to the prison that takes 40% for its own fee and remits the balance to his prisoner account.

David

David hails from Stoke-on-Trent, only about ten miles from Sudbury. He was working as a hairdresser for the years before he regrettably committed two murders and received a life sentence. He is now serving the final year or two at Sudbury and I got to know David well because he was one of the prison hairdressers, and the one I chose to go to. One of the rooms had been converted to a salon with two chairs and all the usual equipment, and of course background music, but not too loud to prevent a conversation. It might seem unnerving to have one's hair cut by a double murderer, but one is comforted to understand that he would not be at Sudbury if he were still considered dangerous. Those murders, a long time ago, were, he told me, committed whilst he was in a drunken rage and for the first time I was quite glad that there is no alcohol at Sudbury – well not a lot anyway. Nevertheless, David is a proficient barber, and certainly a lot cheaper than I was used to outside. All prisoners can have their hair cut, and it is free of charge if booked through the prison system – on the correct form of course. However, it is possible to obtain "private" service if the barber is offered a piece of prison currency, usually a tin of his favourite "mackerel in oil" obtained through the weekly purchase of supplies and extras available to all prisoners. So for a cost of £1.60 a prison haircut can be purchased – very good value. If I could go back just for a haircut, I would.

Alex

Alex, age 21, from Liverpool, is serving a two-year sentence for money laundering. When he was fifteen he set up a PayPal account and received about £7 millions (yes-£7 millions) by advertising Escrow facilities. This was from about 5,000 individuals so the average amount received from each customer was in the order of £1,400. He was acting illegally because he did not check the authenticity of the deposits, and he ought to have realised that the funds were of criminal origin. Of course, no doubt he started his business to provide just such a refuge for funds gained from criminal acts. The prosecution alleged that Alex took a commission – he said that he didn't, but I find that hard to believe. He had been on bail for four years before being charged and the trial process took another year. He has an English father and a Russian mother, and after release he intends to go to Russia with his fiancée to "leave all this behind". He speaks fluent Russian and will probably be one of the next generation of Russian billionaires.

Sam

Sam, aged 48, is getting a transfer to Ford open prison on the south coast to be nearer his family during the final year of his sentence. He had previously lived in Spain on the Costa del Crime and has several businesses, some legal and some illegal he told me. I got the impression that he was very comfortably off and looking forward to enjoying his ill-gotten gains. Sam was in a Manchester bar when he was confronted by another person with a knife. He says that he disarmed the attacker and accidentally slashed the assailant's face. The Court took the view that the response was disproportionate but Sam thought that it served him right. Otherwise, Sam was an amiable sort of bloke but I would not want a disagreement with him – especially if he had had a few drinks. He had a kind side – when he thought that I did not have a hat during a very cold spell of weather, he wanted me to have his. However, I did have one; I just wasn't wearing it.

John

John is an IPP prisoner whom I met in the Chapel one Sunday and also in our French language lessons. Although no longer an option for the Courts, these types of sentence having been ruled illegal by the ECJ, this was formerly a sentence given for appropriate offences when the Judge considered that the accused needed to be held for a minimum period but crucially not released until considered a safe risk for the public. IPP stands for Indeterminate Public Protection. Release is at the discretion of the Parole Board after consultation with the Prison Service and the Probation Service. The Prison & Probation Service is nominally a unified organisation, but whereas the Prison looks toward the release of a prisoner, the Probation Service wishes to be responsible for as few potential risks as possible. John has so far been in prison for eleven years longer that the term originally sentenced for. There are about 3,000 IPP prisoners still in UK jails and without doubt some are the victims of unfair treatment. The main problem seems to be that the prisoner has to prove he is not a risk, whereas, in fairness after the sentence is completed it ought to be the Crown that should prove that he is still a risk. John's position was complicated by him being a citizen of Eire, having renounced his UK citizenship, on advice, several years ago. Anyway, John is cautiously optimistic that he will win his freedom within the next few months. He never told me the exact nature of his crime, but I did gather it was for an extremely violent act, but no death involved. John was a qualified electrician and assisted the contract company in any electrical work throughout the prison at Sudbury and also the nearby women's prison at Foston. I must say that I always felt entirely comfortable with him and never in doubt that he presents no future risk to society. On release, he is going to set up as a self-employed electrician and I am helping him in the formulation of his Business Plan which is necessary for him to apply for the various grants that are available from certain charities to ex-prisoners. His partner and daughter have stood by him for fourteen years – that is true loyalty.

Ahmed

Ahmed, from Kurdistan and latterly from Derby, is in prison for fraud, accused and convicted of selling six million cigarettes imported without paying duty and sold to the public at a loss of £1.25 million to the Exchequer. He was sentenced to four and a half years but was upset because his friend had received a two-year sentence in similar circumstances; the Judge had imposed the sentence because the mastermind behind the operation was still at large. However, since the trial, this person had been apprehended, so Ahmed was hoping for a reduction of sentence on Appeal.

Cooper

I met Cooper from Wolverhampton, age 42, near the end of an eight-year sentence. He has four boys, aged seven to twenty-two, by three different mothers. He has a business in the waste disposal sector which is being managed in his absence by his father and a younger brother. His involvement with crime was brought about by a broken marriage and drift into drug usage. He wasn't short of money but deeply regrets the deterioration in his quality of life, and is now looking forward to being free in six months' time when he is determined to go straight.

Danny

Danny, aged 52, from Boston told me his history. He had spent many years in prison over several sentences, this time for six years on account of robbery. He had been guilty of a street mugging, snatching a handbag from a pedestrian. From the scene of crime, he had sprinted a hundred yards before he collapsed flat on his face from the effect of drugs, and had been arrested on the spot. He told me that he had a history of drug taking and homelessness. In fact prison life was a welcome break between his periods of liberty and stress. At least he was being housed and fed.

Craig

Craig owns a midlands haulage business. He had been sentenced to twenty-six months for tachograph fraud; eight of his fifty vehicles were found to have false tachograph records. His father was the Transport Manager of the company, but as he was 84, Craig had taken the blame. His main concern was a POCA (Proceeds of Crime) claim for £1.2 millions, this being the total income gained by the offending lorries for the time involved – not taking any account of the fuel, driver, or vehicle costs incurred. He is awaiting an Appeal, but his main concern is to clear or substantially reduce the POCA liability.

Amarjit

Amarjit from Birmingham came to see me about a new restaurant that he and two others intend to start. He had written a lengthy Business Plan and had received some provisional offers of funding, and was looking for some more input. It was interesting to work on the plan and inject some commercial sense into it although he has plenty of time because he is not due for release until later next year. Sentenced to seven years, his partner is in a nearby women's prison as a co-defendant in the same case but for a slightly shorter term. The offence was that of fraudulently cold selling timeshares; they had persuaded vulnerable and elderly people that their villas were to be compulsory purchased by the Spanish Government, but by selling now a better price would be achieved - a payment of a few hundred euros now would get it on the market without delay. Before being apprehended the twelve conspirators had received over £1 million in total. Amarjit is truly remorseful, has turned to Sikhism, rid himself of his serious drug addiction problem which had caused major self-harm and bulimia problems, and has fully realised that he sinned, wickedly taking advantage of the vulnerability of old people. He has spent his prison time studying for degrees at the Open University, completely kicking his smoking and drug habits, not by any treatment but by pure self-will, and training to be a motivational speaker to young people and victims of drug abuse. He blames drugs for being in the state of mind that allowed him to be persuaded to join the fraud.

Don

Don, aged 36 now, comes from Matlock in Derbyshire. He has been in prison for sixteen years already, having been convicted of murder. He killed (I do not know how) a friend in his own home and is now serving a life sentence although he hopes to gain parole within the year. He was very sensible about his position and told me that he deserved to be in prison – that is the punishment for murder. He now gets a regular four-night stay out of prison every month, which he has to spend at a hostel in Matlock. He is not allowed home – the scene of the murder – but in any case, his wife has now divorced him. He has relations who have supported him who live near Banbury, and he was interested to learn about my knowledge of the area. Whilst in prison he has qualified as a forklift truck operator and now has a licence, so he plans to make use of that when he is released. He longs for a family life and hopes to get married to somebody one day. How sad. What a waste of a life. Let's hope that he can re-build it at the age of 36 when he gets out. Good luck.

Nadeen

Nadeen asked me to write his story using his true name. He is 37 years old and comes from Dudley near Birmingham. His father and mother came from Pakistan in the 1950s but Nadeen has always lived in the UK. His wife could only come to the UK four years ago and is now keeping house with their two daughters, aged thirteen and two years old. Certainly it is a struggle.

Nadeen, was, in addition to a seven-year driving ban, sentenced to six years in prison for causing death by dangerous driving in May 2015. Amazingly, however, it was another eighteen months before he was tried in court before a jury. Being a taxi driver, he considered himself an experienced driver. Nevertheless, on an off-duty day, he drove out of a side road at 36-mph (in a 30-mph zone) and collided with another car travelling at 57-mph (in a 30-mph zone) which overturned. The driver and her son, who were both wearing seat belts, survived without serious injury, but her neighbour's ten-year-old son, who was not wearing any safety belt, was thrown from the car and died three days later in hospital. I thought it was the driver's responsibility to ensure that all passengers are using safety belts but this driver escaped any charges.

Nadeen knows he was at fault and is very remorseful at his genuine mistake. He does think, however, that he was very badly defended (a very common complaint in prison) and has lost trust in the police and judiciary for what he sees as an excessively harsh penalty. This incident apart, Nadeen is a decent person and I fail to see that keeping him in prison until November next year will serve any purpose. Surely society can think of a more sensible punishment for this type of offence where there was no hint of any malice.

Rasesh

Rasesh told me a sad story. At the age of 32 he is serving a four-and-a-half-year sentence and has lost his professional qualification. He was Financial Director of a company with an international chain of hotels, and is in prison for insider trading. Aware of "inside" information he was guilty of trading shares advantageously. He curses himself for his foolish error of judgement and knows that he has thrown a good career away. However, what good society will exact by putting his marriage in jeopardy and keeping him away from some meaningful employment is not certain. Anyway, we enjoyed playing chess against each other.

Mush

Mush, who came from very near my home in Leicestershire, was serving six years for fraud. He had imported TV box sets into the country – that in itself is not illegal, but he had sold them to provide cost free access to channels. Mush was a full time Orderly in the mathematics department, so I met him twice weekly when I was on duty. Mush is now leaving Sudbury every day and commuting for his work - to Leicestershire.

Lee

Lee joined me sitting on the benches near the bowling green (too uneven for any serious bowling though) at the heart of Sudbury obviously looking for someone to talk to. Although he was eagerly waiting for antibiotics to start working and relieve his tonsillitis he was still keen to tell me his story. He had only just arrived at Sudbury and was intending to apply for work in the gardening department as he is an experienced tree surgeon. He wasn't sure that he would be provided with a chain saw but he said that he would be able to get the many trees around the prison grounds into a much healthier state – removing the twisted, dying, and diseased branches.

He is due to be released on licence next November after having served a forty-month sentence for burglary. Since 1999, when he was 25, he has now had eleven prison terms in 19 years, all for burglary – all private addresses. The proceeds have funded his drug addiction which he told me can cost £100 to £500 per day; even a small cannabis user can probably spend £15 per day or £100 per week. He first got hooked on drugs through a friend who now lives in Cornwall with an excess alcohol addiction, but Lee says that he himself is no longer taking either drugs or alcohol. Outside, he has attended some detox units and various treatment centres which he told me were useful, but in the end you have to want to give it up. Lee is now at that stage and is determined to stay clean and make something of life when he is released. He told me that his past habits had ruined the lives of his parents and his sisters, and that he is truly sorry. He said that he felt ashamed of having stolen other people's property to fund his drug habits. His mother had told him that if he is sent to prison again she will have to wash her hands of him, but they have assured him of a big welcome back in November. Meanwhile he is serving his final months in Sudbury which he thinks is a palace compared with other places he has seen.

Lee wants a fresh start and told me that he is thinking of learning more about Church. I told him that the Chapel service is at 6.00 pm Sunday and that Helen, one of the Chaplains, was well worth talking to. So we agreed to meet again on Sunday. I never saw him again – I wonder if Helen did.

Sunny

Everyone likes to have a good neighbour and we were lucky to have Sunny, just two doors away. So he was often the person to say "Good Morning", but never "Good Night" because he was always early to bed in his single room. Sunny comes from Wolverhampton, just ten minutes from the Wolverhampton Wanderers FC Stadium, and he has lived in that area since birth, some 49 years ago. Coincidentally, on the same day as we discussed his story, there was a TV programme about Enoch Powell, formerly an MP for Wolverhampton, and the fifty years since his "rivers of blood" speech. Happily, his forecast of doom and racial strife has not materialised but Sunny said that he does remember a lot of racial prejudice when he was young. His parents must have been two of the earlier arrivals from the sub-continent in the 1950s.

Before prison Sunny worked as a postman in Wolverhampton but got involved with a fraud involving time-share properties in Spain and Portugal, and he was sentenced to four years for conspiracy to defraud (to serve two years). He admits that he was involved in a dishonest scam on vulnerable people, and he agrees that his prison sentence was fully merited. He has repaid the large sum demanded by the Court, but is clearly of the opinion that crime can pay and that he can look forward to the future with more confidence than he would have done as a postman. He doesn't need to work again – but he is not the sort of person to do nothing. He is too intelligent for that.

He plans to start a business "doing something", and he definitely intends to stay legal and out of prison in future. He is a convivial person but a straight talker, bemoaning that the country has "gone to the dogs". He thinks that Sudbury is out of control and being run by the prisoners. The officers have either no control or are turning a blind eye. He is free of tobacco, drugs, and outside would drink very little, a social drinker and he is looking forward to his release in a few months' time. My only advice to Sunny would be to "Get your hair cut", but I doubt if he will. Come to think of it though, he is charming with it as it is.

I had a very interesting conversation with the Muslim Chaplain, who was also the Managing Chaplain responsible for the overall operation of the Team and the multi-faith Chapel building itself. He is about 40 years of age and came into the Orderlies Room when I was giving a mathematics lesson to Chris, one of the Orderlies. Asking where I was from - Leicester - led conversation to the recent news of a jeweller who had a shop in Leicester. He said that he had just heard that the jeweller had been kidnapped by a gang who were owed money by the jeweller and, no doubt when he was unable or unwilling to pay, he had been killed – in Stoughton not far from where I live. Apparently the jeweller himself was allegedly involved in nefarious activities and this had led to his involvement with criminal gangs. I said that none of this was apparent from news reports on the TV and in the press, and the Chaplain said that it was nearly always the case that there is much more behind the headline than at first viewing. No doubt we will hear all about it when the case comes to trial.

I asked him if he thought that prison "worked". He thought for a while and said "yes and no". Yes, in respect that there is a criminal world with people that would seem to be "bad" and from whom the public needs to be protected. However, after further thought, he said that they came to prison, usually bragged about their crimes, and had access to others where they discussed how to do it better next time and how not to be caught so easily. As for all the other types of offenders he was very dismissive about the benefits of custodial sentences.

I told him of my experience of some who regard prison as a second home, and he recognised that. He had spent some years as a Chaplain at Winson Green Prison in Birmingham and he said that he was amazed by the number of people who had become regulars, with numerous convictions. He said that it was noticeable that as Christmas and the cold weather approached, this number would increase, and some people would be candid that they were preparing to spend a few months in prison with free board and lodging rather than spend nights in the open and on the park bench.

The Chaplain thought that the fault was the Government's whole social policy. The discussion gravitated to politics generally, and it was clear that although he had strong views of a left wing persuasion he also thought that bringing back Margaret Thatcher would be a good idea.

David

I met David from Spalding whilst eating fish and chips for supper on a Friday evening. The chips were bland but passable; the fish must have come from the Dead Sea. David was serving an eight-month sentence (yes, four to serve); his brother is serving one year and his sister in law ten months – all for the same offence brought by the Trading Standards Authority for selling furniture to the public, door to door, under false pretences. The salesmen were offering the furniture at "discounted" prices, which were not discounted at all. David recognised and accepted that their selling technique was wrong. However, I could not see how a prison sentence was considered as an appropriate punishment.

Mark

Mark from Nottingham will return to his job as a Business Development Manager with a concrete infrastructure company working in the civil engineering sector. He is to be released in a month's time after a five-year sentence for fraud but I never did learn the details. However, he had some strong views on the prison system and Category D open prisons in particular. Apparently, only the UK has open prisons; other countries stick to high security, even in Scandinavia where the prisons are better because they are more modern. He would abolish open prisons, they are like b****y holiday camps. They are no deterrent and no wonder that so many re-offend. Make it a real punishment.

Ron

I met Ron, aged 56, originally from Belfast but he moved to Coventry many years ago. He was sentenced to thirty months (fifteen to serve) and expects to be released in about three months' time. He was drunk (I suspect more than once) and punched the landlord causing a minor injury. However, this was his third conviction; the previous two were for drug trafficking, two sentences of four and six years over the past thirty years. He didn't seem too concerned and had a typically Irish sense of humour. He was telling me of men in Sudbury who would regularly leave the prison for a visit to the shops or pub in nearby Sudbury village. I exclaimed that I couldn't understand the motive for taking the risk of doing this. He agreed, but it's "the young ones, they are stupid and think they will get away with it".

Michael

Michael got involved in a skirmish outside a Worcester nightclub. A glass was broken and in the ensuing melée Michael was accused of causing a six-inch gash in someone else's neck. Convicted for GBH and sentenced to three years and two months, Michael is ready to be released. Happily, he has a job to go back to, as a self-employed tree surgeon (yes, another one). He just has to make sure that he still has a head for heights.

Danny

I had spoken to Danny when he appeared in the Level 1 Mathematics class on a Tuesday afternoon and he was genuinely grateful for some guidance on some simple arithmetical issues. Later on I met him outside one morning whilst I was deciding whether it was pullover weather or not. He asked me how long I had to go – only a few weeks now was the reply. And how long have you got, I asked. "I hope to be out by December" he said. So how long have you been here, I asked. "Here three years, in prison for fifteen". Now there are plenty of men at HMP Sudbury who have been in prison for a long time, but here was someone who was nearing the end of a sixteen-year term, and whom I considered rather a mild mannered and pleasant person. I asked him what he had done to deserve that time and murder was the unsurprising reply. He told me that a girl he knew had been raped by one of her relations, and he and his uncle had taken retribution into their own hands, had gone to the home of the rapist, and beaten him up. They didn't mean, and I have no reason to disbelieve, to kill him but Danny landed a punch through the sternum into the heart and that was the blow that actually killed him. His uncle was released last year; Danny, who went to prison at the age of 18 is now approaching 34. Remorsefully, he said that it would have been better to leave it to the police rather than deal with the matter themselves. He has spent the last year in acquiring a range of skills in decorating, plastering, brick-laying trades, and also learning about railway track maintenance. He has been having home visits recently, so hopefully this is an example of where rehabilitation really does work. Good luck to him.

Simon

Simon arrived after thirteen years in closed conditions and was amazed by the relative freedom, the grass and all the trees. However, it only took a day to acclimatise. He is fluent in Italian and French, in addition to English of course. He worked for a major European company, the parent company of a famous UK brand and he spent three days of the week in Milan and the other two in Luxemburg. An obviously highly intelligent person, he is serving an indeterminate sentence for murder. He killed his partner after arriving home one day to find her in bed with another man. He has obviously made his peace with the victim's family because they are supporting him with visits and moral support; in fact he transferred ownership of a sizeable property to the family as an indication of his remorse. He is truly contrite and realises that his action was just unforgiveable. Clearly he just "flipped" with tragic consequences – a crime of passion.

You will have noticed that I have recounted no stories of those in prison for drugs offences. As I said earlier, that is because I have included them in a later chapter specifically on drugs and my proposal for tackling the situation. There was certainly no shortage of such people and I particularly concentrated on speaking to them in order to better understand the nature of the problem.

Many of the stories that I have recounted in this chapter are for fraud related offences. This doesn't mean that the majority of inmates at Sudbury are in for fraud – just that those are the people who were easy to speak to and who were more willing to enter into conversation. And of course the range of fraud offences varies greatly – for hugely different amounts, the extent of any loss to the victim, the nature of that victim, and the degree of appropriateness for a custodial sentence.

Another significant category of offenders is that for motoring offences, usually but not always involving a death or serious injury. Very often alcohol was involved. I spoke to one young man, from Leicester, who was serving a sentence for drink driving but when I expressed surprise that he was in prison he did admit that he had reversed into the police car that was following him. There was another case where the offender had deliberately driven a getaway van into the shop manager who was obstructing his escape following a failed robbery attempt. However, the usual reason for a custodial sentence is dangerous driving and causing a death in the process, which apparently attracts a mandatory period in custody. I believe that the Court should have much more flexibility in cases concerning a motoring death. Some are guilty of a wholly unintentional accident and others to a willful piece of reckless driving causing multiple deaths or injuries. I have already related the case, earlier in this book, of someone who was returning from a family funeral and had an accident that resulted in the death of his devoted partner. Prison was a wholly inappropriate punishment in this case. Leave it to the Judge.

The third category I would list is that of robbery, with or without violence. Again, the range of offence varies from a not very successful house burglar to a sophisticated bank robber - and even one international art thief. As regards the smaller scale property burglars, the cases I met were all fuelled by the need to acquire funds to purchase drugs.

Another category is the person accused of domestic violence. This type of offender was more evident in HMP Leicester, in those cases where the sentence had been of a shorter duration and insufficient in length for the offender to be transferred out of a local prison to an open one. This was usually for a family argument, often against a wife or partner, but in one case a fifty-year-old man who had been jailed for putting his 23-year-old daughter over his knees and giving her a good thrashing. She reported him. The father was not repentant and said he would do it again if his daughter misbehaved (in his view) again.

Murderers were always interesting people to speak to. The ones I met were of course in their final period of a long sentence. They all admit that they committed the crime in a moment of madness and one they have regretted ever since. They are the ones who in general admit that they got what they deserved – perhaps they are relieved that they are still alive themselves.

Another smaller group were those guilty of gun crime. I always felt more sorry for these people because they were usually not aware that what they were doing is illegal in this country. I know that ignorance of the law is no excuse, but it is a reason. Of course, those that used their gun to actually commit a crime would have been arrested and charged with that greater offence.

I was beginning to form some understanding of which prisoners benefit from a period of custody, what that custody should entail, and what measures would be required to reduce the prison population to the level it was years ago, if that indeed is a policy objective.

In the view of the prison authorities there is a clear distinction between those who might use violence again and those who have no history or record of any violent behaviour. I am pleased to report that I fell into this latter category. This difference is reflected in the procedure and timetable for allowing trips or visits out of the prison grounds during the months prior to a planned release date. Offenders who have a record which include some violent action or tendency, and this includes all motoring offenders, need to have at least one escorted outing with a prison officer before being allowed any day or overnight exeats on their own. Such Day or Overnight temporary releases on licence for those with any tendency for violence are much more difficult to be sanctioned, and are often delayed by weeks. The different types of offenders make an interesting comparison.

There is the calculating professional criminal who is quite prepared to serve a prison sentence in return for the proceeds of crime. It is just part of the risk – almost an actuarial calculation. Into this category come the drug barons who probably calculate that five years away in prison is worth the fortune awaiting them on release. This group is definitely there, but they are a minority.

There is another offender, the habitual criminal, who has served more than one term, and usually several. He is often under-educated, from a disadvantage background, and regards prison as a place of living between those periods when he has to look after himself. He is used to prison life and is not unduly concerned. He will just try not to get caught so easily next time.

There is the person who realises that his standard of living inside prison is probably better and certainly less stressful than life outside, in so-called freedom. Prison is neither punishment nor deterrent. In fact it is a lot better than sleeping in the open on a cold night. After all, where else can you get free accommodation, heat, and food?

There is the person who has made a mistake and is serving the sentence imposed by the Court. There is a negligible chance of re-offending.

There is the younger outwardly over-confident offender, probably inwardly nervous about his ability to handle his new colleagues, who is in the early stage of his life of crime, He has arrived at the University of Crime and will be able to learn the more advanced criminal practices. Sometimes he will mature and become less brash during his sentence. Whether he is less likely to re-offend is debatable.

There are the lifers, those who have an undetermined length of sentence and have little hope of exiting in the near future, although of course a transfer to an open prison is an encouraging pointer. Sometimes one wonders if they will ever be in a mental condition to live outside, such is their dependability on the structured lifestyle in prison; they have been institutionalised. Unless they have strong support after release, and after many years that is less likely, life in freedom will be a struggle reduced to living in a prison hostel and with no job. It might well be less comfortable than the prison that has been home for years.

One thing is common to all prisoners. They are all human beings. Each one tells a different story and many have been very open to me in recounting it. Behind some is a failed marriage or a broken home, or parents who were worse than useless. Behind others are a loving wife, family, young children, and a failure somewhere that caused a lapse and the act of unlawfulness. Lack of education which has restricted alternative life choices is a clear indicator, but I found very little evidence of the "world owes me a living" mentality. Many of those in prison are enterprising and ambitious people. In only a very few cases is the individual so obviously evil in his mind-set that he intends to carry out the same or a similar offence in the future. Unfortunately, however, many do offend again and it is this rate of re-offending that should be the primary concern of those in charge of our judicial system.

The Chaplaincy Teams and Religion

I have nothing but praise for the Chaplaincy Teams that I have met both at HMP Leicester and HMP Sudbury. The first Chaplain that I met was the Rev. Robert Gay, whom I subsequently discovered was the Roman Catholic member of the team at Leicester. He gave me a Gideon's New Testament and assured me he was with me for any reason I needed him. The Chaplaincy Team consists of representatives or ordained persons from the Baptist, Buddhist, Church of England, Ecumenical, Hindu, Jehovah's Witness, Jewish, Muslim, Pagan, Quaker, Roman Catholic and Sikh faiths, denominations, and persuasions (please note the alphabetical order). Their job, collectively, is to enable any prisoner to practise his religion and to offer pastoral support at time of need, and of course especially at the commencement of a prison sentence prisoners will be experiencing all the emotions of fear of new circumstances and the future, absence from home, anger or remorse, and of desperation, despair, and doubt. Some will even be suicidal.

Throughout the prison week there is a timetable of services and meetings for all the faiths. There were about twenty in the congregation at my first Sunday morning 10.15 a.m. Service, although this would include a few who had just come for the change of surroundings. Of particular help to me at Leicester were Jill Willetts from the Baptist Church and Helen Stokes from the Church of England. Jill became a telephone contact with my daughter Jane, and I was able to communicate that I was perfectly all right and surviving the initial shock of prison life, until the time that my personal telephone PIN access was operational. The Sunday service was held in the all-purpose Prison Chapel and consisted of a few hymns, prayers, and a talk from the preacher. The sermons were geared to the theme of overcoming life's temporary difficulties and the assurance of God's love. There were also a few outside visitors attending; formerly these people were called members of the Board of Visitors, but they have now been re-titled as Independent Prison Visitors (IPVs). They are the eyes and ears of the Secretary of State for Justice and are there to listen to any prisoner's complaints and make suggestions to the Governor. They have no specific authority, but they do serve a useful purpose.

I was only at HMP Leicester for eleven days, but if I had stayed for the following week I would have witnessed a visit to the prison by the Archbishop of Canterbury whilst on a brief sojourn in Leicester. The last time he was in Leicester was to bury the mortal remains of the last Plantagenet King Richard the Third.

When I arrived at Sudbury one of my first ports of call was the Prison Chapel, a simple brick-built construction with the main chapel area containing about sixty seats, two offices at one end – the west end (actually SW) but that makes it sound rather a grand building, and a few other rooms behind the Altar. One office was for the Chaplaincy Team and the other was an office/rest room for the Orderlies (the prisoner helpers). The other rooms were a Muslim Prayer Room, and another was, I presume, a cloakroom for the Chaplains.

Annexed to the Chapel was a small kitchen and hatch for the service of tea and coffee, and, if lucky, some biscuits or cake.

The first person I met there was John McCay, the Roman Catholic priest. We had a good chat and we exchanged life histories. It turned out that he used to live in Leicester and in fact is still an ardent Leicester City fan, and is indeed a current season-ticket holder. My daughter subsequently saw him getting out of a car festooned with Leicester City stickers all over it and made immediate contact with him in the car park, prior to a visit to see me. John now lives at West Bridgford near Nottingham and acts as a Chaplain at four different prisons, including Nottingham Prison that has attracted so much criticism recently. John became a firm friend, always ready to talk football, religion, or life generally.

As at Leicester, all the faiths and denominations are represented within the Chaplaincy Team and Helen Thwaite, the Anglican Chaplain, also became a firm support to me during my whole time of enforced residence. She had recently returned to work in the prison chaplaincy after a previous retirement; there was difficulty in filling the vacancy and she offered to return. Prison chaplaincy is not every priest's ambition, but Helen said that she actually preferred this setting and found it more satisfying. She is married to another ordained priest with a parish not too far away. Helen is a good singer and also sings in the Musical Society of a well-known public school only ten miles away. I know it well.

Whereas I have changed the names of others in this book, the names of Helen and John are their real ones – no need to provide them with anonymity – they are two of the best people that I have ever met. As the saying goes, they wear their Christianity on their arm.

It was an interesting conversation with Helen and three others one afternoon just after she had returned from a holiday in Northern Italy, including visits to Florence, Pisa and particularly the cathedral at Lasso which she and her husband had visited on Whit Sunday, which in turn led to a discussion on church hymns and music generally. Whilst in Italy, she was aware of the current news of two seemingly disparate political parties attempting to form a government. Much more noticeable, however, was the number of people on the streets either begging or selling their possessions. Over half a million refugees from Africa have arrived in Italy during the past year and this was evident even in the north of the country. Compared with their lives, Sudbury was more like a holiday resort, especially in the hot weather we had experienced throughout May. This led the discussion to prison and the purpose of prison. She was very disappointed that during the years of her work within the prison service as a Chaplain that the emphasis on rehabilitation had virtually disappeared. She said that fifteen to twenty years ago there were many greater options on re-training, behaviour correction and anger management, and courses on a range of subjects than exist today. She assumed the reason was a lack of funding and the fact that prisons are overwhelmed with far greater numbers than previously. The conclusion, not stated but clearly obvious, was that either a significant increase in resources is needed or a significant reduction in the prison population is necessary if the former emphasis on rehabilitation and preventing repeat offending is to be achieved.

After Easter John McCay disappeared for a few days as he was joining a party making a pilgrimage to Lisieux in Normandy, France. The purpose was to visit a shrine to Saint Therese of Lisieux who lived during 1873 - 1897. As a young girl of fifteen she entered the Carmelite Convent there, but unfortunately died of TB at the age of twenty-four. She is remembered particularly for a book on spirituality called *Story of a Soul*; she outlined her relationship with God with three stages – Confidence, Trust, and Daring. She was popularly known as "The Little Flower of Jesus" and she obviously made a huge impression on her fellow nuns and was canonised in 1925 by Pope Pius XI.

I used to attend the weekly Church of England service on a Sunday evening, and also the Roman Catholic Mass held every Tuesday evening. The Sunday service was very broad (some would say rather happy-clappy) in appeal, consisting of a few hymns and prayers, interspersed with talks by Helen. The final part of the Service was a truncated "Story of the Last Supper" ending with the communion of bread and wine. I would sometimes act as a Eucharistic Assistant in the offering of the wine. Pedro, a fellow inmate, acted as organist and provided the musical expertise, such as it was. Helen knew my musical preferences and joked that we would arrange a full Choral Evensong before I left.

The Roman Catholic service which was presided over by Father John McCay was taken from the weekly "Jerusalem Sheet" publication. It lasted about thirty minutes with no hymns, but included readings, a homily (Roman Catholic for sermon), and the Mass itself. I sometimes read one of the lessons. These occasions were always very worth attending and usually concluded with a cup of coffee and chat with those present. There were several who were always there, including Peter, who had converted to Roman Catholicism at a previous prison, and of course the large Irish and traveler contingent. John McCay would join us at the coffee table and sit, smile, and listen.

Both Helen and John said that they really found satisfaction and purpose in carrying out their ministries within the prison service. I was reminded of the words of C.T.Studd, a one-time famous cricketer and missionary:

> *"Some like to live within the sound*
> *Of church and chapel bell.*
> *I want to run a rescue shop*
> *Within a yard of hell"*

The members of the Chaplaincy Team are supported by Chapel Orderlies (prisoners who volunteer to carry out the support work) and are in attendance by rotation throughout the week, morning, afternoon, and early evening. They all do wonderful work and are always ready to listen to and advise any caller. The Chapel building itself is also used as a venue for other activities, which include Bible study classes, prayer meetings, discussion groups, a Saturday evening Bingo session, a weekly "Pub" quiz (without the pub element), and several music groups – some of them rather loud. Drums and other percussion instruments are all available together with the upright piano and electric organ.

It is true to say that a large majority of inmates never cross the threshold of the Chapel door after their first visit, in the first few days after arrival, when attendance is compulsory for a short fifteen-minute induction into what the Chaplaincy Team can offer, and what the Chapel is for. All new arrivals are told of the availability of the Chaplains for private discussion, the procedure for arranging visits, the availability of bereavement counselling, the Listener scheme, the Chapel library, the support available for drug addiction, and preparation for eventual release. The Listener Scheme is the prison version of the Samaritans. Certain approved prisoners are selected to be trained as Listeners, who are available for contact from other prisoners who may feel in need of moral and mental support. In the more extreme circumstances this would be those with suicidal tendencies. The Listeners act as a first port of call and a conduit to more professional support as appropriate, always safeguarding the essential confidential relationship between prisoner and prisoner.

Services at Sudbury Prison Chapel were certainly not in the style that I had been used to. I have always preferred to attend church services presented to a high standard of liturgy and musical accompaniment performed in buildings of historic grandeur, beauty, and acoustic quality. When visiting family in London, for many years I sometimes attended the 11.15 a.m. Sunday Sung Eucharist at Westminster Abbey which I always said was the best musical in London – and rather less expensive than the price of a West End theatre ticket. The music is performed by singers of the highest calibre, who on other days of the week would be performing on stage with some of the country's top choral groups, many as soloists in their own right.

In contrast, Sudbury services were rather different. However, I had the strange thought that Christ himself would have felt at home with a group of prisoners and convicted sinners. It reminded me of the story of the tramp, disheveled, scruffy, and downcast who was outside the doors of a fashionable city centre Church complaining that he had been refused entry by some pompous churchwarden (the type that likes telling everyone how much time he or she spends on church work). He was asked to find somewhere more suitable – when an invisible presence told him "Don't worry, I have been trying to get in there for years".

News has just come through of the death of the world-famous evangelist, Billy Graham, at the age of 99. I remember many years ago going to the Aston Villa football stadium to hear Billy Graham preach during one of his UK tours. It was a memorable occasion and thankfully the weather remained dry. Thousands went forth at the end of the address to sign up as converts, although subsequent research did indicate that very few of these turned out to be more than very temporary converts. Nevertheless, conversions do happen, and I witnessed some.

I have seen examples of men, formerly hardened criminals convicted of seriously heinous and violent crimes and spending early years of imprisonment as drug addicts and unrepentant individuals, stumble on a chance meeting with another individual who suggests a change of course in the path of life.

Scott

I asked Scott, someone as described above, what had happened to him that changed his life. He told me that, whilst in Dovecote Prison, one day he was feeling very low, bitter, drug dependent and despondent, having just learnt news that his wife had left him, when someone else said to him "Don't worry, Jesus still loves you' "Who is this Jesus" he said. To cut a long story short, when he is released in a few months he will take up a place at a Bible College where he will train to become a – nobody knows yet. As he said, "God will tell me". Of course his faith will be tested – it is with everyone – but fingers crossed. He certainly has faith. Let's hope it is not blind faith.

Paul

Paul was someone I met early on in the Chapel. He was approaching the end of a six-year sentence for a violent crime, the details of which I do not have. However, by his own admission, for the first half of his sentence he was a "basket case", unrepentant and with a drug addiction. For some reason, however, after a visit to the Chapel and a chance meeting with a Chaplain, he suddenly decided that he had to start a fresh life. He started to communicate with others, attend the Chapel regularly, learn about Christ and His earthly life, and he became what is sometimes called a born-again Christian. To cut another long story short, on Advent Sunday he was baptised at the weekly service, just two weeks before his release. He returned to his home town of Blackpool where the Church of England Chaplain at Sudbury had pre-arranged support from a local Church. Unfortunately, his flat in Blackpool, retained during captivity, had been broken into, and he also found his pet cat long dead. This was upsetting because he had been assured that the RSPCA had collected his cat when he was first imprisoned and had arranged care for it. However, later reports were encouraging. His previous employer had given him his job back, and Paul was getting his life back on track again. He is now a regular worshipper there and he also helps at a local homeless charity. Good luck Paul, and a real triumph for Helen and the Chaplaincy Team.

It is wonderful and a privilege to have witnessed this sort of conversion, even if I have only witnessed the final acts of these stories. They are truly the modern equivalents of conversions on the road to Damascus. People like Helen Thwaite must be applauded for guiding and nurturing these miracles.

Spending time in prison has given me the opportunity to consider issues of religion and spirituality. Despite the fact that we now live in a multi-cultural society, and prisons are even more so, we are still essentially a Christian country. At least, we have an established Church of England which preserves the relationship of Church and State and ensures participation in national affairs, both ceremonial and in the mechanics of government. You will be relieved to learn that I am not, however, going to commence a discussion on whether the

Church should be established or disestablished.

As John McCay and Helen Thwaite said, prison can be a time of reflection, and I have reflected that in the title of this book. In some ways it is a retreat, and the lifestyle can sometimes be rather monastic. I have not had to reflect on domestic upsets, nor needed to resolve any substance abuse in drugs or alcohol. I did not need to be kept in prison for reasons of public safety (or at least I hope not). I have not been re-habilitated; in fact I spent a lot of time helping to re-habilitate others by teaching mathematics and providing friendly counsel. I doubt if the issue of deterrence is relevant in my case and I would not say that I have been punished. Yes, the loss of liberty has been very inconvenient, but hardly punishment. I have, however, seen a complete other side of life that I would not have seen otherwise. In fact the experience has enriched my life, and it has given me some time to reflect on religion, as structured in the Church of England, and Christianity, which is a very different thing.

I have been trying to resolve my love for the Anglican choral tradition, and my awareness that this is not really what Christianity is about. When we attend a magnificent service in a Cathedral or other historic building, are we attending a Service for prayer and worship – or a Concert?

I will still attend the traditional Anglican choral services, and I hope that the quality of these can be maintained across the country, and not only in those cathedrals that have the benefits of choir schools. The wonderful choral tradition of our cathedrals and major churches is well known and the unique tone of boy choristers as produced in the UK is admired internationally. Unfortunately, this choral tradition is not as alive and kicking as it once was, but it is surviving despite the factors that make life difficult for choirmasters and directors of music. These issues include parents' unwillingness to commit their children to regular weekday practices and Sunday services, that are necessary for any good choir, the many other attractions open to the young people of today, and the much earlier age nowadays that boys' voices do actually "break", which is currently in the 13-14 old age group, as opposed to the 16-17 age group that it was sixty years ago when I was a choirboy. There are also undoubtedly some parents that do not wish to expose their children to any of the horror stories associated with predatory choirmasters that have received some publicity in the past. All these factors are on top of the reduced church going attendance, no doubt caused in part by greater mobility and the ability of families to "get out for the day".

The formation of girls' choirs is a welcome and much needed measure to recognise these issues and maintain a strong musical tradition in our churches.

I don't believe that one has to go to Church in order to be a good Christian. You don't have to be a Christian in order to live a good, decent, and caring life. Christians might say that it helps because Jesus gave us such a magnificent life example and his standards were so wonderfully set out in the Sermon on the Mount. Nevertheless, other religions and none are compatible with a code of good citizenship and caring for others.

I do believe that Jesus Christ lived on this planet 2000 years ago and that the gospels record His earthly existence. The claim that He was the Son of God is a matter of faith and cannot be scientifically proved true or false. It is quite plausible to accept the "big bang" theory for the beginning of time with the acceptance of a greater force speaking to our souls, when we are prepared to listen to it. Some might even describe God as the Great Architect of the Universe. Christ referred to life after death on several occasions – "Today, thou shall be with me in Paradise", he said on the Cross to one of the robbers crucified with him. The exact form of a resurrection will be made known to us at the appropriate time – hopefully a suitably delayed one. I have always considered life as seen on earth as similar to the wavelength spectrum. The colours of the rainbow can be seen, but there are wavelengths beyond the visible out there and yet unseen.

Going to Church of course has a purpose. If you are a member of an organisation it makes sense to communicate with other members. It is a public demonstration which may encourage others to learn more about it. Christ himself often associated with his followers by having a meal, and indeed at the Last Supper instructed us to take bread and wine "in remembrance of me". He said "do this in remembrance of me" not do it if you are doing nothing else today, or do this at Christmas and Easter time or whenever you remember.

So it follows that Christians need to meet as a group in order to celebrate Holy Communion. We do need Church buildings, and the fact that they have been used sometimes for over a thousand years adds to the significance and awe of the occasion. Group gatherings in Church are also good for great occasions like weddings, funerals, and local or national celebrations. The great choral tradition is upheld by the daily Services of Matins and Evensong.

BUT, Christ himself warned against praying in public. He said:

"Do not be like the hypocrites, for they love to pray standing in the synagogue and on the street corners to be seen by men". He continues "but when you pray, go into your room, close the door, and pray to your Father, who is unseen. Then your Father, who sees what is done in secret, will reward you. And when you pray, do not keep on babbling like pagans, for they think they will be heard because of their many words. Do not be like them, for your Father knows what you need before you ask him. This then is how you should pray", and he gave us the Lord's Prayer, the all-encompassing prayer that covers everything, the greatest prayer that has ever been composed.

The early Christians of course were probably dissuaded from meeting too publicly and openly for fear of reprisal, such was the persecution threatened by some authorities at various times in the early centuries. Regrettably, this is still the case in some parts of the world today.

So, for me, prayer is best done in private. Attending Church services is more like attending a concert, and there is nothing better than a good Mozart or Haydn Mass, and even better if accompanied by an orchestra and performed in a building of exquisite beauty and acoustic property. Well-sung responses and psalms (sung at the right tempo of course) are the joys of formal public services.

If Christ were on Earth today I believe that he would feel very much at home in Sudbury Chapel – with all the sinners. After all, Christ said "He who is without sin, let him cast the first stone". Although the music is not brilliant, the message is clear – live life the Christian way. Hate the sin, love the sinner. That is the Christian message. What is the Church of England, or more accurately some of its members, doing about it? I cannot help reflecting on some of my recent experiences.

I was very disappointed at the ordained Minister who did not want to welcome a former offender who had completed his prison sentence from coming back to Church. I was organising a concert at the Church and asked the Minister if he minded if I released a ticket to this former offender so that he could attend the concert which I knew he would be especially interested in. The response was very evasive and clearly geared to avoiding any embarrassment to members of the regular congregation who would also be attending the concert, despite the assurance from myself that the seating would be diplomatically arranged. The response that I received was that it would be better if that person did not attend the concert. I retorted that I did not think that that was the answer Christ himself would have given. The Minister then had to agree with me and told me to arrange the ticket. Unfortunately, a few days later events conspired to cause the ex-prisoner to withdraw and the Minister displayed undisguised satisfaction at the development.

Whilst I was preparing my defence I was also disappointed to receive an email from another Minister of Religion, semi-retired, when he declined to offer a statement to the Court, regarding myself, on the grounds that the Church had advised him not to have any contact with me. If he did not wish to give any testament, then fair enough, be honest and say it. Since when, however, has the Church had a policy of terminating any relationship with those who have sinned. Whereas I would like to thank another retired priest who had no hesitation in offering a similar statement on my behalf; he has given support and advice throughout and acted with Christian motives.

I was also disappointed when the Church organisation itself took over eighteen months to confirm that all the funds I improperly borrowed / took / embezzled (call it what you want) had in fact all been replaced. In fact substantially more had been repaid, but the church was unable to confirm this. Whether this was due to an inability to carry out the necessary accountancy work, or a more sinister refusal to release the truth, I could not possibly comment on.

Yes, and of course I am very disappointed in myself for not resisting what I thought at the time would be a short-term expedient to address a temporary business cash flow situation and treating what was in my responsibility as a bank overdraft facility – a very bad abuse of trust.

Whilst on the subject of disappointment, I am also disappointed in the Archbishop of Canterbury, particularly when he makes asinine comments like the European Union being the greatest dream for human beings for the past 1500 years – since the fall of the Western Roman Empire in the fifth century. He is reported to have said that it had brought peace, prosperity, compassion for the poor and weak, purpose for the aspirational and hope for all its people. How does he reconcile these comments with the fact that the EU foreign trade policy is to put trade barriers up against the world's poorest. How does he reconcile his comments with financial policies that have caused massive youth unemployment and social upheaval throughout the majority of its component countries. In summary, I am a Christian. I am just rather peeved at the Church of England. Maybe I will get over it.

Alistair Campbell, spin-doctor to Tony Blair, famously said that "we don't do God here". Of course, nothing is worse than politicians, or anyone, wearing the badge of religion in any sanctimonious way (as the Pharisees do), but religious beliefs and the policies of putting Christian values and standards into practice must surely be the defining influence for our political and business decisions.

Some people think that Christ would have been the Socialist Member of Parliament for Nazareth East. This is to simplify and misinterpret His teachings. I have always been a One-Nation Conservative, a Compassionate Conservative, and always thought that the State has an important role to play in the direction of resources and ensuring that free enterprise works in practice. My time in prison has given me the opportunity to witness at first hand some human and social problems that any civilised country must tackle with more drive and urgency than is evident today. Politics is about putting your principles into action.

The creation of wealth is best generated by the capitalist system, and indeed it is the capitalist system that has brought billions of people throughout the world out of the depths of poverty over the past thirty years. Nevertheless, the capitalist and free enterprise system will not retain common consent if its effectiveness is only demonstrated by homelessness, food kitchens, crime, and poverty.

I believe that it is the task of the Conservative Party to develop policies that combine the social responsibilities of a caring Christian with the wealth creation objectives of a free enterprising commercial nation. Perhaps I ought to write another book.

Drugs

No account of prison life would be complete without a chapter on the supply and use of drugs. However, I have never taken a drug in my life, excepting of course a few drops of alcohol in very modest and social quantities, a cigar thirty years ago, or of course medication prescribed by a doctor. I have also never come into contact with drugs except on one occasion when a strange smell in the foyer of a ski resort hotel was later identified to me as that of cannabis. I therefore admit that I am no expert on the subject and my comments set out in this chapter can be taken or rejected. Nevertheless, I have seen enough evidence and spoken to lots of people to at least put my thoughts and proposals on paper. Here are some of their stories.

Steve

Steve admitted to me that he was the nearest person to a "professional criminal" that I was likely to meet. He was serving eight years for importing a substantial weight of drugs. Actually, he reckoned that he was sentenced to four or five years less than might have been the case because the police must have "removed" half a kilo on his arrest. His "tariff" was therefore for a shorter term, and he was delighted with the police whom he thought must have taken the missing quantity to sell for their own gain. It was later suggested to me that the difference in the two weights might have been the impurity in Steve's drugs haul. The prosecution will be brought based on the weight of "pure" drugs.

In addition to drugs importation, Steve ran a successful repairs and maintenance business and he had amassed a significant portfolio of BTL properties, both houses and flats. He has been married three times. His third wife of eleven years had warned him, after a previous conviction, that if he ever offended again and was sent to prison again, that she would not visit him. She has kept her promise.

Steve told me that he was approaching retirement age and he would probably call it a day – probably. Steve is not a violent person, but obviously someone who feels unable to live within the law. He was not unduly concerned to be in prison and gave me the impression that he was continuing his business activities whilst in prison, and if he is in an open prison and is willing to risk having a mobile telephone and Internet access, then there is no reason why he cannot.

Kevin

Kevin is in prison for selling drugs, the difference being that he was a very "upmarket" drugs dealer. His customers included stars of stage, screen, and television in addition to some leading barristers and other professionals. No names in this book of course, but he did name-drop a few people. He is firmly of the opinion that the possession of drugs should be decriminalised. He said that nothing is going to stop the use of drugs. His clients all took drugs responsibly; and if any dependency did ever result his clients had the necessary wealth to book in at The Priory for a spell of treatment.

Michael

Michael, age 45, is an Aston Villa supporter, and serving six years for a drugs offence. I met Michael in the Mathematics department where I was able to help him learn to answer some relatively simple questions that most eight-year-olds would have no problem with. He was willing to learn but freely admitted that he had wasted his schooldays and was now regretting it. Michael was desperate to pass his Level 1 examination as this is an essential pre-requisite for authority to take on work outside the prison gates during the final year of one's sentence. I gave Michael some extra tuition on a one-to-one basis so that he could achieve this. He is desperate to be in a position to get a decent job that will enable him to avoid the temptation of getting involved with supplying drugs again.

Asma

I met Asma, a very smart and presentable young man, aged about 40, in prison for importing cannabis. He was sentenced to twelve years (remember that is six to serve) and has done four and a half so far, expecting release later in 2019. I asked him where the drugs came from. Pakistan was the answer, although he said that nowadays they are also coming from Spain and some South American countries in addition to the traditional source of Pakistan, which is of course adjacent to Afghanistan, the world's largest production centre. I asked him if it was worth it. His answer was very much in the affirmative. The wealth he has amassed, and no doubt carefully placed out of reach from investigators (i.e. not in the UK) was well worth the few years of lost liberty. I asked him if he would do it again and his answer was "never say never" but he doubted it. At his trial the Judge had told him that if he ever appeared before the Court again the sentence would start at eighteen years. Although his marriage went through a rocky phase at the start of his sentence, he was pleased that the relationship was now much happier. His wife is looking after their two young children and I got the impression they were being well provided for.

Mark

Mark, aged 52, a diabetic, is in for sixteen years for importing drugs. He has already served six years and expects release in about a year. His wife has left him, but he intends to re-unite with his two children. He plans to start a new business with a friend – complementing the friend who is good at everything except sales, and his own ability to sell almost anything. Providing he can sell the product, and the product is legal, the business will succeed.

Nim

Nim from Leicester was sentenced to six years (three to serve) for drug trafficking. He obtained his goods in the UK and re-sold them to his local customers. He told me that the original price for the drugs would be small, but many layers of profit are added before it reaches the final consumer. He smiled when I asked if he had made a lot of money, but he did say that he would not re-enter the business – it would be too serious for his family if he were caught again. He also told me that he has friends in other countries who have been caught trafficking and who have received much longer sentences – one for 34 years. He has another business interest in used cars and he will concentrate on expanding that business when he is released in a year's time. I asked him what the answer is to the drugs situation in the UK and his opinion was that the position now is out of control and that the police are not making any significant progress in dealing with the problem.

He would legalise all drugs, as that would destroy the high profits being made by the middlemen. He also said that avoiding the dilution of drugs would make them safer, but I am not sure that just making drugs legal would achieve this objective.

Sean

Sean, aged 21 from the Birmingham area, was sentenced to eleven years and hopes to be released within the next year. He had gone to the home of someone who had burgled his mother's house and shot him with a firearm for which he had no licence. The shot was intended to kill, but in fact only injured the target. The police raided his mother's house to arrest him, but Sean escaped through a back door and was on the run for four days. Finally arrested by the police he was found in possession of a quantity of drugs. He told me that he was not actually charged with the drugs offence, a trade that had provided him with a good income of up to £3,000 per day for several months. He had been supplied by a relation who lives in Poland and he had been receiving 60 kgs of hash every week. He also told me that he has three children, the first when he was aged thirteen and after he was released he would have some more – but he did not know who the mother would be. I was trying to teach him some mathematics, but it was not the easiest job to get his full attention.

Tom

Tom was one of the older generation. He was first arrested many years ago for growing cannabis. He said that he grew a lot of it, even having an industrial unit where all the necessary lighting had been installed and suspicions grew when the electricity company noticed excessive usage. Initially sentenced to a few years he stupidly walked out of an open prison and was a "free" man for over ten years. After he applied for his state old age pension (that was his mistake) he was re-arrested and sentenced to eight years. So it has been a costly experience for him, except that he is not short of friends. He had alternate visits from, one week his wife, and on the alternate week his girl-friend, who came with carer and zimmer-frame. I asked him what the answer is to the drug problem. He replied that he was no expert, and that his production of cannabis had only ever been sold to one customer (the middle-man). He therefore did not know much about the criminal side effects of the trade but as regards cannabis, definitely legalise it. It is no different from alcohol, he said.

Mohammed

Mohammed told me that he was sentenced to eight-years (to serve four) for conspiracy to sell drugs in Bradford. He was never actually caught selling them himself but he had associations with others who were. Anyway, he said "never say never" when I asked if he would do it again. He didn't want to do VAT fraud because unlike his friends he did not understand it enough, if at all. Mohammed was my star mathematics pupil (by that I mean the longest serving and most amusing); he kept asking me if I would impersonate him and take the exam on his behalf, but eventually thank goodness he passed Level I on his own.

I have related many case histories of those whom I have met and talked to whilst in prison. There are countless other stories that I have not told, but they all fit various profiles.

There are the serious and professional major drug dealers with strong sources of supply. Many have made millions from their trade. Some of them would say that they are businessmen satisfying a clear demand.

There are the uneducated and the less intelligent who have been caught because of their greed and naivety in avoiding police identification. Typically, they have a few sources that they then supply on to 2-300 customers in their locality. A lost or mislaid mobile telephone is often the lead that the police need to catch them.

There are the "handlers" and "couriers" that have been dragged into the trade, usually to resolve a temporary cash requirement. Some bitterly regret their involvement; they have learnt their lesson and vow that they are finished with drugs forever. Others fully intend to resume their activities as there is no way they can earn £1,000 per day by any legitimate means.

Then there are those caught in possession, not of supplying drugs. These people have attracted shorter sentences and usually serve their time in a local prison without ever reaching somewhere like Sudbury. They are the ones where the damaging effects of drug addiction can often be witnessed at first hand.

There are also many thousands, spread over every city, town, and village in the country, that have not yet been caught, and probably never will be. They are continuing to supply their customers.

Whenever a Judge passes a sentence there is a tariff according to the class of drug – Class A, Class B, or Class C. Also relevant is the amount of the drug discovered, whether the offender is considered to be "in possession of" or to be a "supplier", where the offender and the drugs were found, and of course any previous record. In some cases, police can issue a warning or an on-the-spot fine of £90 if you're found with cannabis.

Class A includes the more dangerous drugs – crack cocaine, cocaine, ecstasy, heroin, LSD, methadone, methamphetamine.

Penalty for possession up to 7 years. Penalty for supply and production up to life in prison.

Class B includes amphetamines, barbiturates, cannabis, ketamine and others.

Penalty for possession up to 5 years. Penalty for supply and production up to 14 years.

Class C includes anabolic steroids, benzodiazepines, GHB, GBL and others.

Penalty for possession up to 2 years. Penalty for supply and production up to 14 years.

Sentences, as illustrated by the stories I have recounted, can vary from a few months to many years. As those who have been convicted of the lesser offences more often serve out their shorter sentences in a local prison without ever reaching the time they might have been transferred to an open prison, those whom I have met and spoken to at Sudbury were those who have been convicted of the more serious offences and received the longer sentences. Furthermore, they were towards the end of the custodial part of the sentence and can look forward to very close monitoring by the Probation Service on release. There are a large number of prisoners who have been convicted of importing and supplying drugs and in every case I spoke to they made large profits prior to their apprehension. POCA (Proceeds of Crime Act) action has confiscated these proceeds, but in most cases I am confident in saying that the amount taken is a modest proportion of the total and that most have substantial sums spirited away and held awaiting their eventual release. Assets in the form of property, jewellery, cars, and bank accounts can be identified and seized with relative ease. Even hidden cash can often be located. The clever ones have funds abroad or held by trusted friends.

These people are not dangerous in the violent sense, but they have been found guilty of selling drugs like heroin and cannabis to large numbers of the general public on the streets, in the schools and universities, and elsewhere. They are therefore responsible for a great deal of misery and unhappiness, together with all the minor crime which is committed in efforts to raise the finance to purchase their wares. Furthermore, most of them can give no assurance that they do not intend to revert to their former work when released. This is for the very obvious reason that it is most unlikely that they would be able to earn anywhere near the same amount by any legal occupation. From discussions that I have had, earnings varied from £1,000 per day to, in one case, £20,000 per day. A daily profit of £3,000 was not an untypical amount claimed to be the "rate for the job". These are enormous figures for people who very often have limited literacy and numeracy. The more intelligent ones will admit that their arrest probably resulted from being too greedy. All know how and why they were caught, and how, if so minded, they will take greater care to ensure that they are not caught again. In general, they do not regret their offences and have regarded imprisonment as the calculated risk for the benefit of earning big money.

Many of these people also told me that if the government legalised drugs that their trade would be sabotaged. I do not agree. Legalising drugs would definitely decrease the profitability of the trade, but it would greatly increase the numbers taking drugs and the total consumption. The response to the problems of drug addiction in this country needs to be more radical; it does of course need to tackle the supply as well as giving treatment to those affected.

The extent of casual drug taking amongst the population in the UK, as in many other countries, is well documented. The reasons for this range from seeking to get "high" and happier to wishing to enhance alertness and stamina – improve performance physically or mentally. Others will take drugs to help tackle depression and all the pressures of life. Taken to excess, this addiction can have harmful effects, and sometimes with fatal consequences. Furthermore, the requirement to generate sufficient funds in order to purchase drugs also leads to other crimes being committed such as robbery and mugging. It has been estimated that over half of all convictions in this country are drug related in one form or another.

In prison, drug taking is rife, in both closed and open establishments. It is the principal reason for inmates being transferred back to closed conditions, but after transfer it seems it is just as easy to continue with the habit. The inability to accept captivity and a restless desire to provide an escape for the mind, if not the body, is an added reason to take drugs in prison, in addition to any addiction that might have been present before conviction. Strangely, those in prison for selling drugs were usually less likely to have a problem with the actual consumption of them.

Drugs are available in all prisons, and to control this is reputedly one of the main security objectives of the prison staff, after stopping any escapes of course. Somehow drugs are smuggled into prison, with the help of family, friends, and accomplices. A few inmates told me that their teams were still operating to supply drugs (inside and outside) despite their own absence, and that their earnings were continuing, albeit at a reduced level. Prison visits by family or friends present the greatest opportunity for passing the substances from one to another, but there is little to stop a package being thrown over the wall, especially at an open prison where the wall is a fence. More devious methods of transfer with a mouth-to-mouth kiss and embrace between prisoner and girlfriend happen, and prisoners have been known to conceal drugs within their bodies in a secure capsule or bag to be recovered at the appropriate time (please forgive me for not explaining in more graphic detail). It is said also that some prison officers are corruptible, but I have absolutely no evidence to support this statement and I very much doubt that this is the case at HMP Sudbury.

An additional problem in prisons is the added incentive of switching from the less dangerous cannabis to the more dangerous heroin. Apparently, the cannabis can be detected in the body for a whole month after consumption whereas heroin can be cleared within 24 hours provided sufficient water in imbibed to flush the body system adequately. The prison staff do conduct random tests on inmates, and specific ones when there is a suspicion, so this provides a regular flow of identified transgressors. One sometimes gets the impression that the scale of punishment for being discovered depends largely on the pressure to create more prison spaces for the influx of new arrivals. I waited in vain for my random drug test.

Based in Derbyshire there is also a special team with trained sniffer dogs that visits Midlands prisons in rotation, and I saw these at Sudbury on two occasions. This was one of the prompts for a rush of spring-cleaning. Suddenly, many of the usual suspects would feel the need to use copious amounts of detergent to clean their rooms. All furniture would be moved into the corridor whilst the floor and shelves were thoroughly cleaned – no doubt with the purpose of removing any traces of offending substances.

There are facilities for treating drug addiction in prison as there are outside. However, the nature of the market and the sources of supply mean that very few of those who might benefit from antidotes and counselling do in fact apply for it. They therefore do not receive any treatment and are not known to the authorities. Of course, one of the main reasons for the prison drugs problems is that a very significant proportion of the inmates have in fact both experience and expertise in the procurement and distribution of all types of drugs. Is it any wonder that they continue with what they know best, identifying those that may be tempted and satisfying their needs. If the pushers and traffickers were removed from the scene, then the drugs problem within prisons may be more comparable to the problem outside. How can we reduce or eliminate the trade in drugs? If we can, then there would be fewer men (and no doubt women) in prison to feed what, by all accounts, is the biggest single challenge to discipline and the safety of prison staff today.

The problem is also exacerbated by the fact that the variety of drugs on the market is apparently much greater today, and that the potency of these drugs is unpredictably variable. Cannabis for example is now sold in many different forms, some much more dangerous than earlier versions of it.

So that is the problem. What is the solution?

Solutions, or more accurately measures to control, have ranged from even stiffer sentences for those convicted, much more effective policing of the sources of supply, to legalising the supply and consumption and providing much better treatment facilities and education. I do not think that legalisation of drugs, even just Class B and C, is the answer.

I am going to make some proposals which I fully appreciate some will regard as outrageous, unworkable, and crazy. They may be right, but I will proceed to set out what I would do in the unlikely event that I would ever be in a position to implement it.

I appreciate also that others will criticise my policy as smacking of the "big brother" technique and the nanny state. Furthermore, why should the drugs trade be treated any different from tobacco or alcohol. However, cigarettes, tobacco, wine, beer, and spirits are already subject to taxation and are already only available from approved or licensed premises. There is also an age restriction on the ability to sell and purchase. The supply of drugs is out of control and the current position presents a clear and obvious danger to the health and well-being of the nation, particularly its young people It is also putting an unacceptable stress on both the ability of the law and order authorities and also the health and social care authorities to cope with the situation.

We need to destroy the drugs industry as it is presently operating. The best way of ruining any industry is to nationalise it. I would therefore nationalise the import, production, and distribution of all defined drugs, and any variations of these. Leave the legal definitions to the experts.

A new organisation would be formed – sorry, another Quango – I have called it the National Drug Supply Authority (NDSA). It would be a national monopoly, with sole authority from Parliament to import or produce in the UK a full range of drugs required by the market. It would also have sole authority to supply these drugs to approved outlets. It would remain illegal for any private individual or business to supply drugs and similar penalties would apply as at present.

End users of drugs, members of the public, would be required to register as a "Licensed User". The immediate benefit of being registered would be to confer on the Licensed User the status of being free from prosecution or penalty for the possession or consumption of all drugs. This would include hardened addicts to casual participants. I know that this registration process would be a big job and take time, although not as long as all that. The immunity from prosecution would in itself be a huge incentive to register. The greater benefits would follow.

The registration of Licensed Users will be as confidential as possible and the register will not be for public availability. However, it will involve disclosure of name, address, and any contact details, so the User can expect to receive communications from time to time. Each User would be issued with a User Card (the size of a Credit Card) which would need to be presented and swiped whenever a purchase was made. No card – no purchase. The card would indeed need to contain some photo ID and the more recent fingerprint technology would be a further improvement. There would of course be a few who still considered their personal anonymity as paramount and chose not to register (maybe a famous TV presenter) but that would be his or her choice. They would be purchasing their supplies from illegal sources and acting illegally in its consumption.

The User Card would automatically record and store the date, type, and quantity of any purchase, and this data would be available to the User. In appropriate cases, advice and the offer of treatment could be made to the User with a recommendation to make contact with a Local Advice Centre. Users would be advised if their consumption was increasing or decreasing and there would be a host of supportive and advisory information. In the event that any User needed medical treatment, access to the patient's drug consumption history would be available. Greatly improved identification and treatment for Users, including all addicts, would be made possible. In time, overall consumption could be managed downwards.

All drugs would be sold only by the NDSA through authorised outlets such as chemists and such other outlets as approved in order to provide a comprehensive nationwide service. The setting-up of this network would be no more difficult than the rolling out of the National Lottery outlets was several years ago. Obviously, a strict requirement would be the security necessary for safe storage of the products, but drugs would no longer carry the extortionate black-market value that they command today. Delivery to these outlets would be by approved security firms, much as cash dispensing firms are serviced today. Approved outlets would have to purchase their products from the NDSA – purchasing from any other source would be illegal. As supplies from the NDSA will be the cheapest there will be no incentive to do this anyway.

The quality and standard of all drugs would be regulated and managed by the NDSA. This would in itself help to combat the major problem of new and more dangerous versions coming onto the market. Different strengths of these various drugs would be available, but the quality and safety of them would be controllable and continuously improved.

The NDSA would be able to purchase or produce the required drugs at a fraction of the price that Users currently have to pay on the black market. Even after administration, storage, and distribution costs the prices to the Approved Users would be considerably less than the current "market" prices which are inflated by large profit margins being made by a succession of "middle men" involved today with the network of suppliers, handlers, and couriers. My understanding is that it is not unusual for one dose of drug to change hands seven or eight times between the original manufacturer or farmer and the final end user.

With the quality and supply of all drugs being managed solely by the NDSA, the import and sale on black market terms would be undermined as Users would be able to purchase legally and at significantly lower prices through the official outlets. It would remain illegal for any non-NDSA approved outlet or entity to conduct any trade in drugs.

I believe that these proposals would undermine the business model of the current drug providers. They would only be able to continue to service their clients at greatly reduced sale prices, and why would any end-user not choose to purchase from an Approved Outlet and gain criminal immunity.

The supply of drugs by the NDSA would be subject to a dedicated tax. This would not be Value Added Tax as the regulations for this tax would be inappropriate. There would be ample margin between the NDSA cost price and the retail price for a Drugs Tax, some of the proceeds of which would be used to finance Government expenditure for the costs of the complete programme. The costs include purchase, production, transport, security, and retail of the total range of products in addition to the central monitoring and support services for the Users.

The whole programme would be self-financing as the tax levied would be calculated to meet the full costs and more. The Exchequer would have no excuses. In fact, the Drugs Tax would be an extra source of revenue. It has been estimated that if drugs were taxed at the same level as the rate we now tax the drug called tobacco, a sum of £3.5 billions would be raised every year. I don't know the basis of calculation for this assertion, but that is serious money.

A secondary benefit of these proposals would be a very significant reduction in those convicted of either supplying or being in possession of drugs, and this would result in a reduction of those being sent to prison for these offences. Personally, I would take a liberal view when considering those already in custody for these offences, particularly if there were an absence of any violence. The adoption of these proposals would substantially reduce the opportunity and incentive for current drugs offenders to re-offend; they are not generally dangerous men in the violent sense. Furthermore, a reduction in crimes associated with drugs would also be achieved. Acts of burglary, fraud, and violence in order to provide funds necessary for the purchase of illegal drugs would be significantly less, as the cost of the legal drugs would be considerably reduced, such are the exorbitant profits being "earned" today from the trade. Even the cost of these purchases to registered Users could be subsidised providing the User was a co-operative participant to a programme of detoxification and treatment.

Most current users realise sooner or later that taking drugs is harmful to their health and pocket, and would like to be rid of their habit. They need a Government to grasp the mettle, take a big initiative, and adopt these proposals.

The improvement in national health, productivity, and general well-being would put the benefits of Brexit into the shade. I hope you agree.

The Criminal Justice System

My time and experience gained at both HMP Leicester and HMP Sudbury has given me the opportunity to consider, probably for the first time in any depth, what is right and what is wrong with the Criminal Justice System, at least as far as I have gained some exposure and knowledge of it.

The first observation concerns the Police and the CPS (Crown Prosecution Service). I had thought that my own time between arrest and sentence of twenty months displayed a high degree of inefficiency, but I was amazed that this is by no means exceptional, and that many cases take even longer to come to Court. In one case it took a period of five years. I appreciate that there will be reasons that can justify some of these delays, but more usually it is just rank inefficiency. In my own case, I had fondly imagined that the delay was caused by the police checking my assertion that all the funds taken had indeed been replaced. It was therefore with some surprise that I learnt many months later that this fact was not accepted. Clearly no work on this issue had been undertaken and the police had done nothing whatsoever to progress their enquiries. The authorities might say that the cause of this general problem is pressure of work or lack of resources, but the real explanation is lack of any ability or will to make a decision, especially when it can be filed and deferred to a later date - rank inefficiency. Justice delayed is Justice denied.

Similarly, the Court system would appear to be in need of an overhaul. I attended various courts on at least four occasions – twice should be sufficient. A visit to any court building, criminal or civil, will demonstrate the scope for efficiency savings in the scheduling and listing of cases to be heard, the waiting around by not only defendants, but by witnesses and the legal personnel. Judges seem to think that the courts are there to fit in with their lifestyles, not that they are appointed to serve in the country's interests towards the efficient administration of the law of the land. Anyway, enough of the courts, what about the sentences they pass.

There are four reasons to send a convicted criminal to prison for a custodial sentence. The first and most obvious purpose is to protect the public and to remove someone from the streets, and therefore eliminate the opportunity for that person to re-offend. This of course includes those found guilty of such crimes as murder, grievous bodily harm, rape, and robbery but also, notwithstanding the proposals set out in the previous chapter, at least for the present, those found guilty of drugs related offences. Drug traffickers are not usually guilty of physical assault but they are responsible for a great deal of physical harm.

A second purpose of imprisonment is to re-habilitate prisoners, teaching those who have been found guilty of illegal or unacceptable conduct to be able to return to live in society and lead a productive life without the desire or need for future criminal behaviour. One way of measuring this is the reoffending rate.

The third purpose is the old fashioned one of punishment. This reflects the public demand (or at least that of some of our newspapers) for offenders to lose their liberty as a penalty for breaking the law. Another expression is "serving one's debt to society". Some people might even contemplate "Lock them up and throw the key away" or "Let them be punished". Unfortunately, if that is what you want, the prisons of today do not punish, although they certainly remove liberty. Is punishment the same as public vengeance, or has it some higher moral purpose? If it is vengeance, then that is not a very Christian attitude - in fact it is a very unchristian attitude. This is one of the reasons I have always been sceptical of victim statements, believing that justice ought to be dispassionate and not swayed by the ability of a victim to show emotion, very often as a veil for thirsty retribution. Does punishment actually do the offender any good? I am reminded of the schoolmaster saying "This hurts me more than it hurts you". Punishment is only of value if the offender takes the opportunity to challenge himself and make appropriate changes for the future. As the chaplains said, in an earlier chapter, prison is the opportunity for reflection.

I suspect that punishment is why Judge Carr sent me to prison, not to keep me off the street as I am not a violent person, nor to rehabilitate me, as I have spent most of my time trying to rehabilitate others. She wanted to punish me. Have I been punished? Has it been my family that has really been punished in dealing with the aftermath? Well, I would not have chosen to be away from home for several months, but it has been a very interesting experience and I have learnt a lot about life and the "underclass" that I would not have been exposed to at home. Life at Sudbury is perfectly bearable. So, after the initial shock, the exercise is really a waste of time. The reputational damage is effective on conviction, perhaps a lot earlier. There is no need for prison for a significant number of those inside.

In recent years prisons have become places of diminished punishment. Nobody who has been to prison would need to fear going back there as far as the conditions are concerned. Of course they are not good, but they are a lot better than a majority of the world's population have to endure on a daily basis. Conditions at an open prison are certainly not punishment. They may be an enormous inconvenience and waste of time, but hardly a punishment.

The fourth reason for sending someone to prison is that of deterrence. There is clearly some justification in society wishing to deter others from committing the same or a similar crime, but in fairness to the accused the punishment should still be proportionate to the offence and not in any way vindictive. Moreover, it is debatable how effective deterrence is. Very few, if any, think of the consequences before they transgress. Hardened criminals do not think they will be caught, or if they do they regard it as a calculated risk. The murder rate has not changed much despite the abolition of capital punishment. Crimes of passion do not take account of the consequences. The real deterrent is the certainty of capture.

Different Justice Secretaries have had different priorities in their interpretations of these four policy objectives in framing their penal strategies. The prison system used to be controlled by the Home Secretary, but when the Home Office was adjudged as "not fit for purpose" in 2007 the responsibility for prisons and the judicial system was hived off to the new Ministry of Justice. It was Prime Minister Blair's attempt to "Europeanise" our justice system.

Michael Howard, when he was Home Secretary, famously declared that "prison works", thus initiating a dramatic rise in the size of the prison population. Since then different Justice Secretaries have tended to be more liberal, but still inconsistent in specifying priorities. In the past eight years there have been six Justice Secretaries, hardly likely to produce a period of stability to allow the multiple problems in the Prison and Probation Services to be addressed. The Howard League recently said that "keeping its citizens safe, protecting and promoting the rule of law is, arguably, the most important role of government, although apparently not for this government". That might be unfair criticism, but the fact is that since 2010 Kenneth Clarke, Chris Grayling, Michael Gove, Elizabeth Truss, David Liddington, and now David Gaulke have all been Justice Secretary.

David Gaulke is moving in the right direction. He has announced a major overhaul of education and employment support such that prisoners have a job to start the day they leave prison. He recognises that the key objective is to cut the re-offending rate, which costs victims and taxpayers an estimated £15 billions per year (don't ask me how that is calculated). He is giving prison governors greater freedom to decide on the classes offered to inmates so that they can be given skills tailored to the needs of local employers. The Government is also trying to expand the number of major employers in schemes to offer work to ex-offenders. He knows that half the prison population enters prison with the English and mathematics abilities of a primary school pupil, while only 53% have any qualifications at all. Their lack of education, coupled with a criminal record, makes finding work difficult and contributes to the figure of one in four reoffending within the year.

It was Michael Gove who said that every released prisoner needed three things – somewhere to live, something to do, and hopefully someone to love. Well, we cannot do much about the third priority, but it is well within our capability to ensure that the first two objectives are met. In fact, if we cannot do that we may be wasting our time in trying to solve our prison problem.

If I am to advance the argument that I think prison is an over-used penalty today I also have to admit that other forms of punishment have steadily reduced in number over the years. Capital punishment has been abolished, at least in this country. To oppose capital punishment on Christian grounds is to accept that earthly life is finite, and therefore I do not oppose it on those grounds. However, capital punishment creates martyrs and doesn't stop murders. Corporal punishment is no longer considered acceptable in either the school or post-school setting – although sometimes it might be quite a good idea. We no longer have transportation to Botany Bay, and we do not subject anyone to public humiliation in the village stocks. In addition to custody, we appear only to have fines and community service as penalties that the Courts can use as a sentence, and fines are often inappropriate because they do not easily reflect the ability to pay and can often punish family and children more than the culprit. There has been a lot of work aimed at providing suitable work opportunities for community service, but clearly much more is required if the courts are to be persuaded that this represents appropriate alternatives to that of custody.

Certainly, the UK seems to like to send people to prison because the proportion committed to a custodial sentence is higher in the UK than in virtually all other advanced countries with the notable exception of the USA. If there has been a more recent willingness to award suspended sentences rather than one of immediate custody then it has not really been reflected in reduced numbers which currently total approximately 83,000, male and female, but mostly male. This is actually a short-term reduction from over 90,000 during the past seven years, but the number is expected to increase again and plans to accommodate up to 93,000 are in hand. One reason for this is that non-custodial sentences are falling out of favour with judges and magistrates amid concerns about their effectiveness. Another reason is the increase in violent crime attracting longer sentences – last year it surged by 21% with 1.3 million offences recorded by police, the highest level since records began 15 years ago. The current number in custody compares with only 68,000 just 15 years ago.

The increase in prison population has also been caused by a greater number of terrorist associated offenders – the lull after the IRA gunmen has been replaced by others with Islamic fundamentalist persuasions. Some would say that this growth has been caused by the UK interfering in Iraqi and Eastern affairs, but then other countries who have not taken any military action overseas have also been attacked by terrorists, perhaps even more than the UK. Another cause is the recent increase in the prosecution of sex offenders, often for crimes committed many years ago. The Police have even wasted valuable resources by working on allegations against people who have been dead for years.

Keeping dangerous or potentially dangerous people off the streets in order to ensure that normal members of the public are safe from attack or robbery is the only known way of achieving that objective, so there would seem no alternative to prison in these cases. A modern society would probably wish to ensure that these people are held in humane conditions, consistent with the necessity to avoid escape from custody.

Those who were sent to prison primarily to protect the public, by removing them from circulation, progress through the prison system over the course of their sentence. Sentences below four years qualify for release after half has been served and release on temporary licence can be agreed in advance of that; those with a sentence over four years may also gain early release subject sometimes to the approval of the Parole Board. Without doubt there are some dangerous and unpleasant people in detention, and plenty more that obviously have a very short temper and are easily aroused, particularly when drugs or alcohol are contributory factors. In these cases there would seem to be no alternative to a custodial sentence. The younger ones are generally the more menacing ones.

However, even the worst offenders can grow up and improve their behaviour. The calculated risk of allowing potentially dangerous criminals a degree of personal freedom during final periods of a sentence – in an open prison – seems to be a measure of a decent society and is recognition that however bad someone has been in the past there will come a time when everyone ought to be given a chance to redeem themselves. There need to be, and there is no reason to believe that it is not the case, careful reviews of all prisoners to assess their suitability and lack of risk before transfer to open conditions, and regrettably there will always be some that cannot proceed to this degree of trust. Transition through the various stages of security level is the responsibility of the prison organisation and staff of the 121 prison establishments in the UK. Once in the open prison system, progress is recognised by day release, overnight release, home curfew release, and by release on licence.

Unless these sentences for those convicted of a violent offence, against people or property, are to be infinite, the presumption must be that the prison also has a duty to help rehabilitate the prisoner such that when he is finally released he is able to resume his place in society, lead a law-abiding and useful role, get a job, earn some money, and hopefully establish, or re-establish, a happy family life. If only it were that easy. The fact that it is not is proved by the re-offending statistics. It is easy to prove anything with statistics and reliable figures are difficult to ascertain, but one statistic reported that 35% of released prisoners are convicted of another offence within the year. The percentage of Sudbury inmates convicted of another offence is apparently significantly higher. Ministry of Justice figures for 2015-16, the latest available, show that nearly two-thirds of offenders sentenced to less that twelve months in jail returned to crime within the year. Comparisons with the past are difficult because the basis of the MOJ's method of calculation has varied. However, by any yardstick, the figures are deplorable and are a cause of great concern. They also point the direction in which policy ought to be targeted if a permanent improvement in the prison numbers and a reduction in committed crime is our goal. Reoffending costs Britain around £15 billions a year – the equivalent of asking every family to pay £630 – but what the basis of calculation is I am not sure.

The prisons do some useful work in the rehabilitation of its temporary residents, but it is too little and inadequately targeted. In many cases it also has insufficient time in which to bring about any worthwhile change. One major problem is the number of young men in prison for a first offence. Except for the more serious offences it is debatable if anyone ought to go to prison for a first offence, where these young men immediately mix with several hundred others, murderers, burglars, drug traffickers, fraudsters, and thugs. They have arrived at the University of Crime – Sudbury Campus. They will speak freely with those who wish to brag about their prowess and wealth, they will be able to learn more tricks of the trade, and they will learn the most useful advice - how not to get caught next time. Young men who have been sent to prison for a serious driving offence meet with hardened criminals. Crime is glorified.

During my time at Leicester and Sudbury I have met hundreds

of fellow human beings. These have included dozens of young men who, given good mentoring, training, and direction, could be saved from a life of crime, repeated spells in prison, and huge cost to society, both financial and social. These men, who sometimes look more like boys, are being well trained by experienced gangsters and drug traffickers.

The prisons do good work within the resources available to them. Rehabilitation takes many forms, medical, social, educational, training, and the provision of some work experience. Medical care includes treatment for on-going illnesses and particularly addiction to drugs, alcohol, and even tobacco. Social rehabilitation includes arranging for a bank account, recovering a lost national insurance number, providing personal identification documents, perhaps a passport, a driving licence, arranging accommodation on release, and setting up a future relationship with a probation officer. Education offers some elementary training in the three Rs – reading, writing, and arithmetic. Training is available in a range of trades which will provide a qualification in one or more skills that may be the gateway to a job. Work experience provides just that, at least for a few hours every day. Work both indoors and outdoors in the gardens ensures that prisoners have to get out of bed in the morning, arrive at work on time, and participate in work conditions probably for the first time for a long time. Very few of the inmates I met had been in full-time employment prior to their arrests.

At both Leicester and Sudbury, in co-operation with the Milton Keynes College, a range of English language and mathematics courses are available. These are principally at Level 1 and Level 2, for those who understand what is included in this. The mathematics syllabus includes topics like addition, subtraction, multiplication, division, brackets, negative numbers, decimals, fractions, formulae, bar charts, pie charts, graphs, weights, length, perimeters, areas, capacities, volumes, angles, shapes, means, averages, ranges, proportions, probabilities, percentages, approximating and estimating, recognising equivalences, money, time, the international clock, temperatures, and the use of a basic calculator. There was one "pupil" who was very keen, and we progressed to some problems requiring the use of algebra, and some simultaneous equations.

At Sudbury I had the opportunity to offer my services as a mathematics and English mentor. This was both in a classroom situation where I was assisting the Milton Keynes tutor by moving from desk to desk in order to help anyone who appeared to be struggling, and also in one-to-one situations outside the classroom. Most of the "students" were keen to learn, fully aware that they had wasted their schooldays, and needed to learn some basic skills before release and some hope of a job. A few would display little interest or willingness to learn. It was always a triumph when one of these people would crack and just begin to show a flicker of interest. Often this was started by a conversation –

What part of the country do you come from?

Do you support Everton or Liverpool? (other options are available)

When are you going to be released?

Have you any family to go back to?

What are you thinking of doing when you are released?

Of course, nearly every job today requires some ability to write, read, and do some basic adding up. Sometimes the prisoner would say that the only job he knew how to do was to sell drugs, but usually this attitude would soften over time.

Sometimes the attitude would be "I've got a job as a driver when I am out, so why do I need to add up". The best response was – When you have arthritis and cannot drive a van any longer, you might want a sitting down job for a few years. It was interesting work, but one thing I did decide – I would not wish to be a full-time teacher.

The general standard of those attending was worryingly low. This is an indictment of the schooling that these people have received when younger. There is of course an excellent incentive to at least reach Level 1 in English and mathematics as the prison regulations stipulate that only those with Level 1 qualifications can take an employed position outside the prison during their last year. During this final year of a sentence work outside can be arranged and some prisoners can attend nearby towns to take a paid job.

At Sudbury, it is also possible to receive training in a range of skills that might be useful after release. These include bookkeeping, business studies, and IT. I myself attended a Domestic Cooking Course, and apart from eating the production learnt some new recipes. Another course was for a professional cooking qualification and work experience in the nearby Secret Diner café was available for those with security clearance.

Other programmes run by Milton Keynes College at Sudbury specialised in French polishing, plastering, painting and decorating (including wall-papering), and work on railway track maintenance. There was much interest in the track maintenance course, no doubt in anticipation of HS2 passing through the region. Those that I spoke to who had been on these courses told me that they were useful, albeit at a rather less intensive level than would be experienced in any out of prison apprenticeship situation.

It has to be said that some good rehabilitation work is carried out in prison. It is just a tragedy that thirty and forty-year olds have reached this stage of their lives and still need some basic education. Does prison rehabilitate its inmates? The various educational and work opportunities certainly fill some time, the one item that there is always plenty of in prison.

Milton Keynes College do a good job and they undoubtedly try to "process" as many students as possible. In fact the College's income from the Prison Service is likely proportional to the throughput. However, judging by the poor standards it is clear the programmes do little to more than dent the problem. One reason is that in many cases the inmate is not at Sudbury long enough to make any significant improvement in basic skill level.

There are approximately 500 inmates and 25 arrivals and departures at Sudbury every week. The average stay is therefore about six months. In practice, allowing for lifers and those on long sentences, the majority are held for a shorter time than that, and these are the very people who would benefit from some serious intensive education.

Prison life is not generally conducive to rehabilitation. All male company brings out the worst in human behaviour and life in those conditions does not teach anyone how to look after oneself or one's family. Oddly, some of the regulations actually make the process of rehabilitation more difficult. Access to the Internet is not allowed – but who can learn to live in a modern society without knowing how to make online applications, particularly to Government departments and for job applications. I realise the security problems, but it should not be beyond the wit of the MOJ to find a solution to this.

In summary therefore, I do not think that there is any evidence that prison rehabilitates more than a very few people and certainly the degree of re-offending would indicate that it does not. For any significant improvement the prison population would need to be held for longer spells, in better conditions, and segregated according to the type of treatment or training required. For this to happen, a substantial investment in new capacity and personnel is required, and because this would demand heavy expenditure it is not going to happen, such is the pressure on the public purse.

The other alternative is to adopt policies that bring about a substantial reduction in the prison population such that current resources, financial and personnel, can be directed in pursuit of a dramatic improvement in the outcomes for our judicial system. In due course, the requirement for fewer penal establishments would mean that the older and more expensive to run buildings (like HMP Leicester situated on prime city centre land) can be closed and the land sold off for redevelopment and housing, and new purpose-built establishments can be developed or converted from existing facilities. I need to demonstrate how the total number of prisoners can be halved within a short time. Some people would disagree with this objective and think that prison, even in its current state, does work. – and even if it isn't working, it's not worth doing anything about it. I disagree.

My conclusion is that the courts must use the option of a custodial sentence as an absolute last resort. They would probably assert that this is already the case, but I have met many tens of inmates both at Leicester and Sudbury who would have been better punished or dealt with by an alternative type of sentence. If I have met tens of people, there will be thousands in that position throughout the country. Admittedly, the resultant increase in non-custodial sentences would require an expansion of the Probation Service to deal with the greater number of curfews and community service orders. This would be financed in the course of time by a reduction in the cost of the prison estate.

Prison should be reserved for violent offenders who are a physical danger to the public. Except in a few cases, non-violent offenders should be punished by non-custodial sentences and community service. A new policy on drugs would have the effect of substantially reducing the numbers convicted of supplying them together with other drug related offences. A liberal attitude should be adopted with those nearing the end of their sentences once the incentives to re-offend have been removed with the new policy. Add to the above a more enlightened and determined social policy to remove the blight of homelessness and rough sleeping, which are both factors which increase the prison population, and which are a stain on our national reputation. The objective should be to reduce the prison population to below fifty thousand within five years.

The situation demands a long-term strategy to tackle the position before it gets worse. This requires cross-party co-operation so that changes in national policy do not occur at five yearly intervals.

Do you say: "Here, here" or "What a load of rubbish"?

Family, Friends, and Conclusion

Being in prison can be a stressful time and even more so without the support and help of family and friends. It is certainly a situation when one learns who your true friends are, and particularly those that live out Christian qualities of life rather than just profess it.

I would like to record my absolute thanks to my wife for standing by me. The biggest divide in prison is between those whose family are giving support and those who have lost this huge advantage. I also thank my three children and their spouses for their utmost support, and particularly for the past two years. The manner in which the three "children" stood up to the challenge of organisation and support has been superb. It makes me proud that they have been so strong and resilient when it would have been easy not to be so. Not only were they concerned to ensure that all members of the family were coping with the situation, they were also worried about the effect that prison might have on my own health. They found the early days especially very fraught, but they all fell into their respective roles and worked together even better than beforehand. Grandchildren and other family members (well, nearly all) have been magnificent and I hope that I can repay their support and many kindnesses. We always did have a very close family; it is even closer now.

I have said earlier in this book that prison had "enriched my life" and it is true that open prison is not much of a punishment. However, I do not wish to underestimate the pain and anguish that my family have suffered as a result of my misdemeanours. It was worse for them. It is said that the worst day of the week on which to be sentenced to prison is a Friday because the prison system shuts down for the weekend. It doesn't actually; every day is much the same. However, its contacts with the outside world probably do shut down, and I know it was a problem and concern for the family that they knew little about my whereabouts or circumstances for a few days. Apart from a brief telephone conversation paid for by the prison, it was necessary to wait until my telephone charge code was operational, probably four days after arrival. The problem then was access to a telephone kiosk and the ability to hear the other end above the background noise of the prison life at Leicester. At Sudbury, of course, this presented no problem, and there was no shortage of opportunity to ring home or any other pre-authorised number.

At Leicester there was a very efficient system of prisoner emails. Through the website "email a prisoner" it was possible to send an email and pre-pay for a response – the hand-written reply was scanned and emailed back to the sender. Unfortunately, at Sudbury there was only the facility to receive emails. Representations to the Governor were made that it would be sensible to offer the full receive and reply option, and the Governor did respond to me that this was "being looked into" and it was their intention to offer this in the near future. However, nothing happened – at least for the five months until I left. This full email facility would do a lot to improve family contacts, and particularly with those family members who are not able to visit, such as younger grandchildren, or for the younger inmates probably direct contact with older grandparents would be advantageous. Daytime visiting hours are not suitable or possible for many.

I said earlier that on being "sent down" I at least knew what I was in for. However, that was not the case for my family. For me, I knew what I had to deal with. My family were left to start an unknown chapter, sorting out affairs at home and trying to fathom the workings of the judicial and prison systems. They found the Friday date a distinct disadvantage as it was difficult to make contact with anyone who was able to advise on when and where they could visit, what they could bring to me, and to find out how I was. The conflicting advice and lack of any clear instruction was a problem and could be a chapter in itself – but not written by myself. The longer-term prospects for any appeal against the sentence, on the grounds of diabolical representation (was he really a barrister?), were unknown and it was difficult to obtain any sound advice. Many hours of research on the internet were spent, and this situation would have been considerably more difficult for families with less tenacity and ability.

They were concerned about my health and ability to sustain a period in prison, and particularly for the diet. They were right to believe that the diet would not be good, but it is not a threat to health in the short term, although of course it is bound to impact on the health and temperament of the inmates as time passes.

Special days are the visiting days, and great opportunity for exchanging domestic news and views. In fact, it has been said that I was a lot more conversational during these visits than I am normally. A full two hours of conversation over a cup of tea and a snack (even a toasted ham and cheese sandwich) are more than I have had for years. In fact, the catering arrangements during visits improved significantly during my time at Sudbury. Visiting at Sudbury is allowed on Wednesday or Thursday afternoons, and also two sessions on a Saturday and Sunday morning. Bookings have to be made by the visitor(s) in advance and are restricted to once per week for each inmate. It was always interesting to see the wives, partners, or girl-friends and particularly the many with young children who thought the large room was wonderful – plenty of toys to play with.

I asked my family what their impressions of both Leicester and Sudbury prisons were. Leicester was much better than they expected, especially for a building that looks so austere from the outside. It has a remarkably pleasant visiting area, albeit that the interim rooms were grim. They found that courtesy to the prison staff was reciprocated by helpful kindness from the officers. Oddly, it took longer to gain the trust of the staff at Sudbury although once achieved they too proved most courteous and friendly. One of my daughters undertook the role of visits organiser and she found Leicester more amenable to accommodating reasoned requests than were Sudbury. On visits, they were saddened by many of the stories they heard which were a real eye opener and they also commented on the number of families that were obviously enjoying the fruits of ill-gotten gains; they had never seen so many designer clad children.

Just as I explained earlier that there was a camaraderie amongst the inmates, there was also a similar bond of association between the visitors. Exchanging stories and getting involved in conversations whilst going through the various security stages of gaining admission to the prison had some value to my family, and just as they were recipients of useful tips of advice in the early weeks, so they were able to take on this role themselves in due course. They spoke to many other families who were dealing with young children, and some with special needs, who had travelled long distances to be at Sudbury. My family were fortunate in being able to spare the time and being able to afford the transport costs of regular visiting, but with some families this was a big problem, sometimes necessitating an overnight stop and long journeys by public transport. The travelling time, time spent waiting around for security clearance, and the visiting time itself all add up to a considerable commitment for the visitors. Having a family member in prison is an isolating experience at the best of times, as it can be a hard thing to talk about, so the long-term fall-out of trying to cope alone, and then readjusting after release, is significant. Prison is very unlikely to improve the circumstances of any marriage, and because the inmate becomes used to conditions where his prime consideration is to look after himself, it is unlikely to improve prospects for the future relationship. I have said that prison today is not real punishment, but it certainly is for the families, and that is further evidence of the inappropriateness of custodial sentences for certain crimes.

Even better, of course, were the home visits allowed towards the end of the custodial period. I know some of the inmates found these difficult, especially the return to Sudbury after an enjoyable weekend. As I explained early in this book, having been used to periods of twelve weeks at a stretch away from home in the past definitely made me more resilient to this emotion. There are of course always highs and lows; prison teaches you not to be impatient. Just keep busy.

I would also like to thank those friends who have written to me and visited me during this period. Many other expressed a wish to come, but frankly it would have been at the expense of a family visit and I thought it was simpler to wait until "je suis liberé" (or should I use the subjunctive tense). I hope that friendships can be renewed over the coming months.

Has the experience changed me? I don't know. I do intend that it will. Time will tell.

I hope that you have enjoyed reading this short book, relating my reflections whilst away. It has been what is described in the literary world as a vanity project. Frankly, I do not expect to sell many copies – but I have enjoyed the process of writing it. It will probably be one of those books where there are more copies signed by the author that those unsigned.

I would like to thank my daughters and my son and his wife for reading the drafts and giving me their frank comments and suggestions. In my original draft I had included a chapter on Brexit. The comment from more than one person was that Brexit was really off subject from prison and in any case my contribution might well be completely out of date before anyone had read it. My response to that is Brexit was certainly one of subjects I reflected on during my prison stay. In fact I spent much time listening and reading about it. It is, after all, the predominant political issue of our time. It concerns the very future of our nation and the outcome will affect our grandchildren much more than it will affect those of my generation. We have taken the decision to leave the EU on behalf of the younger ones – in a few years' time they will be thankful. I have therefore decided to include the chapter on Brexit as an appendix - hopefully that satisfies everybody.

Thanks to the wonderful CreateSpace programme. I do not have to commit to print a minimum number of copies, but can rely on Amazon to print as any order is received – one by one. Well, I shall order a few copies. I have solved a few Christmas present problems.

I would not have chosen to spend a few months away in

prison, but it has provided an opportunity to enhance one's life experiences and to mix with many people it has been an honour to meet.

Appendix

Brexit

You may ask quite properly what on earth has Brexit got to do with prison. On the face of it, of course, not much. Certainly, Brexit is not the most important topic of conversation in prison and in fact no one ever mentioned it without me introducing the subject first, and I only did that with the utmost discretion. Far more important topics included penal reform, the criminal justice system, police corruption, and the latest football results. Manchester United was the most popular team, especially for non-Mancunians. Those from Manchester, and there seemed to be a lot for a Midlands prison, as always supported Manchester City; everyone from outside Manchester supported United. For those who did have an opinion on Brexit, views in favour of Remain or Leave followed very much the trend of outside – a majority in favour of Leave – but above all a desire to now get on with it.

It was a period of frustration that I was not able to debate the issue with more regularity. My exposure to the Brexit debate has therefore been restricted to reading letters and articles in the Times and Telegraph, and listening to such TV programmes as the Daily and Sunday Politics, Andrew Marr, Peston on Sunday, and of course Newsnight and Question Time. This all adds up to a good deal of regular political digest, but it is not as good as being able to send an email to your MP, write a letter to the Editor, or, even better, to tease ardent Remainers with stories about the undemocratic European Union and its unelected Commission leaders, particularly Jean Claude Juncker, Donald Tusk, Michel Barnier, and the European Parliament's Guy Verhofstat.

Following Prime Minister Theresa May's speeches at Lancaster House and then in Florence, which both set out Brexit strategy in quite general terms, there appeared to be a period of drift when little progress was being made, and opponents of Brexit appeared to be getting more press coverage than the Government. The majority of people accepted the Referendum result and just wanted to get on with it. Opinion polls have continued to indicate a majority for leaving, and indeed the Project Fear campaign forecasting recession and higher unemployment immediately after a Leave vote has been shown to be groundless. Many criticisms of both Remain and Leave campaigns can be made, but undoubtedly the Leave majority would have been significantly higher without the Project Fear propaganda peddled by George Osborne and his Treasury mandarins.

According to a new report published in Standpoint magazine the Treasury's anti-Brexit predictions during the lead-up to the EU Referendum were wrong to the tune of £100 billions. Project Fear, spearheaded by George Osborne, the former Chancellor, was a "giant error" and a "gross miscarriage of government". Mr Osborne's scary rhetoric about a return of the Great Recession now looks preposterous, says Timothy Congdon, an economist and the report's author. He said the difference between Project Fear's forecast and reality amounted to 4.6% of GDP. Instead of employment falling by hundreds of thousands it has risen by hundreds of thousands. Instead of house prices going down, they have gone up. Even public finances are better than at any time since the recession of 2008. Project Fear, it said, was "a mixture of malice and ignorance, of wicked politics and trashy economics – but more cock-up than conspiracy".

Of course, it does not help to have the BBC and Sky News, the Civil Service, and much of the Establishment, so Europhobic in its closet campaign to derail Brexit. BBC presenters disguise opinion as news, and prefix every positive development "despite Brexit" and any negative news as "because of Brexit". Nobody voted to become poorer. Agreed, however we did vote to regain control of our laws, borders, and money – but there is absolutely no need to assume or accept that we will be poorer in the process. Meanwhile, Bank of England and Treasury officials regularly release new forecasts predicting less growth than otherwise might be the case in fifteen years' time, pretending that their long-term forecasts are any more than vague predictions usually founded on inaccurate assumptions. The old computer adage of Garbage In = Garbage Out is all too true. If doubt on their ability to forecast longer term growth is needed, one only has to look at their short-term forecasts that are adjusted up and down every quarter with monotonous regularity. Instead of saying "we're leaving so how do we minimise the damage" we should be saying "we're leaving, so how do we maximise the opportunities".

The Prime Minister's speech at the Mansion House, held there because bad weather had prevented her journey to Newcastle, certainly added some much needed detail to the Government's plans and set the scene for the negotiations with the EU on a proposed Free Trade Agreement (FTA) – we thought. This speech re-affirmed that it is not the intention to remain in the Single Market or the Customs Union. Indeed, retaining membership of either would be incompatible with leaving the

EU – a fact that was clearly spelt out by all the leading speakers during the Referendum campaign, from both the Remain and Leave sides.

It is a pity that the false assumption that an adverse financial effect of Brexit has not been countered by the Government with more vigour. Too many Remain supporters have been allowed to get away with their statements that the different versions of Brexit are merely choices of least bad options. There have been insufficient voices setting out the positive benefits and opportunities that will be presented, such that there need be no adverse financial effect at all. After a relatively short period of volatility the future is a good one.

It does not, of course, help to have a Prime Minister who finds it difficult to say how she might vote if the Referendum was re-held. Her excuse that this is a hypothetical question because there is not going to be another Referendum is unconvincing. Other former Cabinet Ministers have declared that they have changed their minds, and would now vote Leave, have nailed their colours to the mast, and it is a shame that the PM does not do likewise. Certainly, it would be dishonourable for her to lead a Government in a policy which she did not believe in, merely on the pretext that "this is what the country voted for".

The Government must start proclaiming that leaving the EU will bring positive financial and non-financial benefits, always of course on the assumption that the British people and British companies exploit their natural enterprise and initiative, and grasp the challenges. We will become (again) an independent country managing our own laws, borders, and economy. In one word – sovereignty.

Mrs May deserves some credit for the recovery from a disastrous General Election result in May 2017, which was caused by her own lack of charisma and electioneering skills, and also by some "own goals" in the Conservative Party Manifesto which included new proposals which had been neither fully thought through nor properly discussed and analysed beforehand.

However, we are where we are, and at the time of writing I had assumed that no useful purpose would be served by the Conservative Party changing Leader now, although it may be necessary before the next General Election scheduled in 2022. Later events were to change my mind.

Do you remember the red bus with £350 millions committed to the EU every week and suggesting that the NHS could do with some of it? For the record, no one ever suggested that all £350 millions could or would be diverted to the NHS – the figure stated by Boris Johnson and other leaders of the Leave campaign was £100 millions per week – equivalent to £5 billions per years. Remain zealots used to quote "what was on the bus" as an example of lies by the Leave campaign. We have not heard that accusation much recently because the Government has indeed announced massive extra spending for the NHS, much more in fact than the amount mentioned during the Referendum campaign. The complaint now is that this is not due to any "Brexit dividend" because Remain enthusiasts claim there won't be such a dividend. Some of them even think that Brexit is not going to happen.

Anyway, the latest calculation of our gross annual contribution is in fact now £428 millions per week. This is approximately £22 billions per year, and after that proportion which is received back into the UK in the form of grants, subsidies, and other payments, represents a net expenditure of over £10 billions per year – and increasing. It has just been announced that our contribution for 2017-18 was £800 millions more than it was in 2016-17. The Government has guaranteed that subsidies to farming, research, and regional support will all continue for a period until arrangements to suit the UK better are put into place. When we finally leave an amount in the order of £10 billions per year will be available for programmes that our own Parliament will vote for, and I am confident that the NHS and Care will be a prime contender to share these funds.

Cynics say that there will be no financial dividend through leaving the EU, but that is on the unproven assumption that the size of the economy will reduce and that tax revenues will shrink. I do not accept that assumption. I believe that the new impetus for British industry and commerce to go out and sell more to the rest of the world will increase the national wealth. We must maintain the level of sales to Europe, and expand our non-EU sales, assisted by the negotiation of new FTAs over the next few years. Only the doom merchants insist that we will lose European sales and not benefit in other markets.

The Government is (was) planning to negotiate a Free Trade Agreement (FTA) with the EU27. It realises that it will not be exactly the same as membership of the Single Market and Customs Union but it can still be a comprehensive agreement to facilitate tariff-free and frictionless trade <u>and</u> services as it would be unacceptable to include goods (balance of trade adverse for the UK) and exclude services (balance of trade in the UK favour). To cherry pick one without the other should be non-negotiable. The EU must be under no illusion that a deal on goods is not available without a deal on services. That was the Government's position before Mrs May changed her mind.

In the event that the EU is not able to agree an FTA, it would be for ideological reasons, putting the sanctity of the European project for uniformity and a central bureaucracy above the obvious interests of its peoples. In that event we need not fear moving to WTO (World Trade Organisation) rules. We already trade on WTO rules with most of the world, including the USA. Trade Agreements are not a pre-requisite of being able to do business with any area or country. They may help and facilitate, but they are not essential. They help to focus joint marketing initiatives. The success of British industry and commerce will depend, as ever, on the skill and assiduity which they display in their exploitation of foreign markets. We need to produce the right goods and offer the right services at the right price, of the right quality, at the right time. That is the secret of commercial success. The Government's Industrial Strategy is intended to provide the proper conditions in which British entrepreneurship and innovation can succeed, the best training, infrastructure, and support facilities.

As the balance of trade in favour of the EU27 is more than £80 billions per year it is hugely in the EU's interests to conclude an FTA. Indeed, if that were not the case the amount of duty collected on EU imports to the UK would exceed the amount of duty payable by UK customers in the EU by about £7-8 billions per year. This would provide additional funding to the Treasury.

However, sense will prevail, and the best option is to agree a comprehensive FTA for goods and services with the EU27, and the fact that we commence in a position of complete conformity and regularity of tariffs and standards must be a huge advantage and time saver in the negotiating period. We must also be free to negotiate FTAs where appropriate with other countries of the world and the USA, China, India, and particularly the Commonwealth appear to be the front-runners. These FTAs must be to promote the general principle of free trade but not at the expense of unfair trade of subsidised or sub-quality access to the UK market. It will remain our decision whether we accept chlorinated chicken on our supermarket shelves. Domestic producers can be exposed to international competition, but not sacrificed on the altar of free trade if that is also unfair trade. So we must not rush into hasty agreements, but we must adopt the policy of "Global Britain" and set an example to a world that is demonstrating some isolationist tendencies

After all, free trade has brought billions of people throughout the world out of poverty over the past thirty years and the history of trade protection is not a happy one.

There is no reason why the UK should not be able to negotiate FTAs more quickly than the EU has been able to. The EU has been hampered by the need to satisfy 28-member countries with different priorities, whereas the UK will have to negotiate only on its own behalf, in its own interests, and will be able to identify common objectives and mutual benefits with greater clarity and speed.

In its relationships with the EU and the other five continents the UK needs to be speaking with one voice. It is time for Sir John Major, Tony Blair, and Michael Heseltine to stop making negotiations more difficult by undermining our unanimity of purpose and supporting moves to reverse the clearly expressed will of the people. It is amazing that the objection of some "Remoaners" has been that Parliament is not being properly consulted. These are the same people who have been content to see our laws determined in Brussels for the past forty years but who now seek to delay or frustrate Brexit by championing Westminster.

Support for a second Referendum is a disguised endeavour to bring about the reversal of the decision to leave the EU. If the matter does eventually need to be confirmed I believe that it will be in the form of another General Election, and precipitated by a Government inability to pass its EU related legislation through the Commons and / or the Lords. In that case I am sure that the people would confirm their previous decision, but with a much increased majority.

The public would be exasperated that the will of the people was being thwarted. The intransigence of the EU leaders would be evident to all. Project Fear would not wash a second time and the clear path of the EU towards a super-state – a United States of Europe – would be for all to see. A large majority of the UK citizens do not want to be part of this. In fact there is good evidence that majorities in several other countries think likewise.

We are leaving the EU. We are not leaving Europe. We seek a sensible, co-operative, and friendly relationship. Furthermore, we would like to support and contribute to some of the pan European projects that exist and have often pre-dated the EU itself. These include Euratom, the Erasmus University swap programme, and of course Europol and other security co-operation. The Prime Minister has said that commitment to defence and security is unconditional.

Other debate concentrates on the need for and length of any transition or implementation phase. This is only necessary because we have wasted so much time already since the Referendum in June 2016. The Government only recently committed resources to active planning for a "no deal" scenario. The term "no deal" is incorrect actually because WTO is a very good deal. However, many of the system improvements, such as greater capacity to deal with incoming container and freight traffic, will be required regardless of whether we move to WTO rules or agree an FTA with the EU. We need to make this interim period as long as necessary but as short as possible. It is best in any change situation to make that change as decisively as possible once the decision to change is made. Delays cause doubt and lack of certainty. Investment decisions get delayed and put on hold. Let's get on with it.

It should also be remembered that we have agreed to plug a hole in the EU budget by contributing about £39 billions more than we are legally liable to. The EU must be reminded that "nothing is agreed until everything is agreed". I hope Mrs May remembers this as well.

There are four other important issues that require some urgent clarification. These are immigration, Northern Ireland, agriculture, and fishing.

During recent years the rate of net immigration has been running at a level equal to the size of a medium size town every year. Is it any wonder that the supply of educational and health services has been stretched? It has also been a contributory factor in the problems of adequate housing supply. Moreover, much of the increase has been as a result of migrants from Eastern European countries who have (apart from helping to fill the prisons) undermined the position of the less educated workers in the UK.

Immigrants are welcome and fulfil a vital role for our country, and it was undoubtedly a big mistake for the Government not to make its position clear at the outset that, regardless of the negotiations outcome, those already in the UK would maintain all their existing rights, and will remain valuable and welcome members of our community. Very belatedly, Mrs May has now given these guarantees to everyone already here, but it was a missed opportunity not to do this at the outset.

We must have an Immigration Policy that is nondiscriminatory and does not favour the Romanian worker against the Indian doctor. As Global Britain we must be open to those from our Commonwealth friends as well as our newer ones from Eastern Europe. However, the total number allowed to settle in the UK must be subject to a ceiling determined by the Government and approved by Parliament, arrived at in the light of all the relevant information.

We do need to attract some foreign workers, both skilled and unskilled, to guarantee sufficient labour for our industry, commerce, and service sectors. At the present time this would appear to be particularly for nurses and carers for the NHS and care system, and fruit and vegetable pickers for our farms. The latter can be catered for by a Seasonal Workers system. We must also ensure that entry is hassle-free for students to attend our world-class universities, one of our best export earners, and of course tourists and other short-term visitors.

However, we also need to train our own unemployed and provide a literate, numerate, and hard-working force of men and women to challenge the import of lower cost foreign labour, which many firms have found the easier option. Firms should be able to satisfy their labour requirements but a fee to obtain a work permit might be a positive encouragement to provide good training for UK personnel. Cheap EU labour has been one of the reasons for lack of training for the indigenous population. Increasing the cost of low skill employment will also encourage the introduction of automation and other productivity improvements.

It is disappointing that over a year since the Article 50 letter was sent to President Tusk that the Government has still to publish its proposals for a New UK Immigration Policy – and not even yet a Green Paper for discussion. Meanwhile, the uncertainty for people and business is only harming our ability to prepare for the new frontier.

The position of Northern Ireland and the need to maintain an open border between North and South is the problem that opponents of Brexit hope will cause the negotiations to fail. All parties wish to maintain the North / South relationship which was enshrined in the Good Friday Agreement of twenty years ago. If a tariff free FTA is agreed, and if it is not it will be because the EU does not want it, then the problem would be entirely soluble, of which the pre-authorisation of regular and local movements would be a feature.

It has already been the case that the specification of any product exported from one country to another has to conform to the country of destination, the importing country. So goods moving South would conform to EU standards and need to certify as such. Border controls would not be necessary. Any testing, no doubt on a random basis, could be carried out nearer the end-user.

Similarly, any Eire goods, or goods from the EU passing through Eire, would need to conform with UK standards if exported to Northern Ireland or even direct to Scotland, Wales, or England. The UK Government has already guaranteed that no border controls will be put in place, so any other controls would be elsewhere, if at all. As both the UK and Southern Ireland are presently producing to the same set of quality standards, it is very doubtful that this would ever become a significant problem.

The real problem is the historic but undeclared ambition of the Dublin Government and Sinn Fein members, north and south, for a united Ireland. That will only come about if a majority in the North vote for it. Otherwise it must be resisted. Mrs May has allowed the EU and Ireland to elevate the border issue to unwarranted importance.

The Common Agricultural Policy (CAP) has improved since the days of wine lakes and butter mountains, but it remains a system of support designed to support originally French farmers, but nowadays also those from Spain and Italy. Subsidies are principally geared to supporting agriculture on the basis of land owned, and in this country the higher payments are made to those larger landowners and already wealthy people. That cannot be right.

Michael Gove has promised to design our own UK Agricultural Policy with the emphasis on land guardianship and animal welfare. We look forward to some detailed proposals which need to be introduced with the support of the farmers themselves. The objective must be to improve the proportion of home consumption being produced in the UK, to facilitate and incentivise the expansion of UK food exports, and to foster all the environmental and animal welfare issues. All these policy objectives will be much more achievable as an independent country,

Fishing of course was the industry that Edward Heath sacrificed in order to complete the accession arrangements when we joined the former Common Market in 1973. No wonder that the fishing communities voted overwhelmingly to Leave in the 2016 Referendum. It is worrying that the Transition Agreement recently published has continued the arrangements to fix quotas until the end of 2020, but the Government has assured the industry that after the transition period we really will be in control ourselves.

The ability to re-charge our fishing industry by claiming a much greater proportion of our own waters will regenerate not only the fishing industry itself but all of our coastal areas which have seen so much deterioration during the past thirty years. I hope also that a new UK Fishing Policy will give incentives to fishermen to not only catch fish and maintain the "correct" stock of fish in the sea (whatever that is), but also to help clear the seas of waste and collect the billions of tons of plastic that are currently polluting the waters around us. That would be a positive policy and one worthy of government financial support.

Recent press reports have indicated that much of the UK's current quota has been sold to foreign firms, with a subsidiary in the UK, who have proceeded to land the fish abroad, often in Spain. The Government must ensure that the benefits of increased quotas are felt by those working in the service industries here in the UK.

It will be good to regain complete control of our trade policies which are often negotiated in tandem and in conformity with our foreign policy. At the current time, the Common External Tariff, a constituent part of the Customs Union, dictates that imports from third countries (i.e. non-EU) are subject to tariff barriers. These import duties are collected by the EU member country at the point of import and forwarded to the EU, less a small commission for handling and administration. Our own consumers are therefore paying higher prices for imported goods than they would otherwise need to. I am not proposing a blanket tariff free offer for every country in the world – that is for negotiation when we conclude new FTAs. However, there are many instances where our own industry would not suffer if some of the import duties were reduced or eliminated altogether. We no longer have a significant textile industry but our consumers pay an 11% duty on imported clothes from China and all the other countries that appear on the labels of the clothes we purchase on the high street and online catalogues. Our own textile industry is now more specialist and less price sensitive than it was a generation ago and would not suffer from this measure. An immediate reduction in the cost of clothing would be brought about. The poor would benefit most and the funds saved would be spent on other goods, providing a fillip to those other industry sectors.

Likewise, the UK is not a big producer of oranges – and many other foods. However, we place a duty on the import of oranges from third world countries and farmers from France, Spain, and Italy benefit from this protection. The Secretary of the British Sandwich Association (an august body) has ridiculously said that after Brexit there might be a shortage of tomatoes to put in our BLT sandwiches. Well, if Spanish farmers don't deliver, I am sure that Moroccan farmers will. Would it not be better to remove the duty on the African imports and give the benefit to the UK consumers? World food prices are reputedly 11% less than EU food prices.

The common External Tariff is a most unethical policy – some would say lacking in any Christian morality. Furthermore, it is much better and more sensible to support third world countries by giving them a market in which their farms and businesses can expand their exports to the UK rather than just handing out foreign aid. Reductions in particularly clothing and food prices for the UK consumer would also benefit the poorer here in the UK and thus help to address our own social inequality problems.

Foreign policy was never a function of the EU, but it now has a Foreign Policy Commissioner. Unfortunately, it has demonstrated a lack of experience in its early foray into the area of foreign policy. It plans to initiate it's own EU Army, which will be in direct competition for resources with NATO, the organisation that can claim responsibility for the existence of peace in Europe since the last World War.

EU foreign policy has been principally responsible for awakening Russian fears and isolationism with its simplistic courtship of Ukraine and other border countries. Opportunities to engage Russia have been lost and the outcome is a potential new Cold War with Russia being more estranged from its European neighbours than for many years.

The Euro currency has been a disaster with a "one currency fits all" policy for a wide spread of economies from the northern states of Germany and Holland to the southern Mediterranean countries of Italy, Spain, Portugal, and Greece. The result has been high unemployment and shamefully high youth unemployment. Meanwhile, the single currency has been very good for German industry that now runs a huge trade surplus with the rest of the Eurozone. In order to finance this trade Germany is lending more and more, and the other states are borrowing more and more.

All currency unions need to have a system of transferring resources between its constituent areas, from the richer regions to the poorer regions. This happens in the United States of America and also in the United Kingdom. The EU only has a mechanism for transferring very small sums between countries and Germany will not agree to any relaxation of these rules.

The EU leadership realises that the only way of correcting this imbalance in the Eurozone is to achieve further integration in respect of tax, financial control, and banking union – "ever closer union". The assets and liabilities of each member state must become the assets and liabilities of the entire Eurozone. The borrowing of each State to finance its own overspending must be controlled by the central authority.

This of course is why some would wish the EU to become a United States of Europe. This may be acceptable for some countries, many of whom have no history of independence and others who do not mind submerging their national identity within a larger super-state. We in the UK have over one thousand years of national history to celebrate and preserve.

So, for all these reasons I firmly believe that leaving the EU will prove to be the catalyst that will Make Britain Great Again, and that in ten years' time we will wonder what all the fuss was about.

I thought that what I have written broadly encapsulated the Government policy so well expressed at Lancaster House. Unfortunately, our Prime Minister, assisted by a civil servant called Oliver Robbins (no doubt shortly Lord Robbins), has chosen to concoct a hybrid offering which has become known as the Chequers Agreement. Several Government Ministers have chosen to resign rather than support it.

The Chequers plan has some merits. It would mean that we would definitely leave the EU and the process of "ever closer union". We would take back control of immigration, but the suspicion remains that our future immigration policy would be heavily influenced by EU demands, and we would stop paying vast sums to the EU.

However, it offers a common rulebook for trade and ignores services which is 80% of our economy. In practice, this means accepting EU decisions without any representation. It will restrict our flexibility in negotiating FTAs with other countries and it proposes what is called a Facilitated Customs Agreement which involves us collecting duties on behalf of the EU.

There is considerable doubt that this Chequers Proposal, as set out in a 98-page White Paper, which you will be relieved to learn I am not adding to this book as an appendix, will be acceptable to the EU. It is certainly not acceptable to the EU

Commission, although Mrs May is was hoping to by-pass it by negotiation directly with leaders of the constituent nation states, a plan that appears to have failed. It is also doubtful that the Chequers Plan will be accepted by the House of Commons, although if it were agreed with the EU, it might just persuade enough MPs to support it. Rather than bring a finality to the European question which has dogged us for thirty years, a settlement based on the Chequers Agreement would continue it for another ten years and delay our progress and recovery from the current uncertainties.

More recently still, the Government has just published its European Withdrawal Paper which includes its Irish backstop conditions and which many regard as impossible for any sovereign country to accept. In any event, it is unlikely to be approved by the House of Commons – but we shall see.

In recent weeks Project Fear Mark II has commenced. The problems of cross border supply chains, just in time manufacturing, frictionless frontiers, queues of lorries at Dover, shortages of medicines, food shortages, potential violence at the Irish border have all been the subject of scaremongering by Remainer groups. All of these issues are soluble given determination, energy and creative thinking.

The situation is a very fluid one. A majority of MPs do not want to leave the EU without an Agreement of some sort, although continued intransigence by EU leaders might change a few minds. It is difficult to imagine that Mrs May could survive as Prime Minister if her plan was rejected. We need a Government which will negotiate a comprehensive Free Trade Agreement (a Canada plus plus) on the lines of the Lancaster House speech. If that is not acceptable to the EU, then we need to give notice that we will trade with them on WTO terms and retain the planned £39 billions earmarked for the EU in order to cushion short-term volatility here in the UK.

I think that another General Election will be held before long and that the Conservative Party will be led by a new Leader. By the time you have read this we will know if I was correct.

Printed in Great Britain
by Amazon

16408684R00092